A MARRIAGE
made in
HEAVEN
BUT GOING THROUGH HELL

Pastor John F. Ramsey, Sr.

POWER PUBLISHING

Indianapolis, IN

A Marriage Made in Heaven But Going Through Hell

Pastor John F. Ramsey, Sr.
Dr. Al Long, *Contributing Editor*

ISBN-13: 978-0-9842874-7-5
ISBN-10: 0-9842874-7-7

Library of Congress Control Number: 2011913789

This book is manufactured in the United States of America.

Power Publishing
13680 N. Duncan Drive
Camby, IN 46113
(317) 347-1051
www.powerpublishinginc.com

Cover Design: Parada Design

TABLE OF CONTENTS

INTRODUCTION

God intended marriage to be a wonderfully, blessed institution (Genesis 2:18-24) that creates an intimate, honorable, and permanent bond where both the male and female raise and nurture children in a household centered in love and mutual respect, only dissolved by death. While this definition gives a perfect foundation of what to expect in marriage, let's face it, while marriages are made in Heaven, unfortunately many couples are literally going through hell!

Marriage was created by God to bless both individuals their children, and both sets of families. However, many couples feel as if they are simply surviving day-to-day, going through the motions of living and not being able to imagine getting to the "death do us part" piece. In the first chapter I will go into some of the startling statistics on marriage that we all hear, but don't seem to digest. So therefore, it is important to find ways to successfully live a life within marriage that supports creating and sustaining a loving and happy home for everyone involved.

With alarming divorce statistics even within Christian homes, wouldn't you think it was a better choice to repair your marriage before throwing it aside? Most people would rather get something new than to repair what they have. There are some situations involving abuse, a hardened heart, and several others that may result in divorce. However, there is nothing that is too hard for God to resolve, restore, or reconcile. You may feel that your situation is hopeless, but rest assured that there is hope of living a balanced and healthy life within the confines of your current marriages, and to live life with your current spouse as God intended. This book will not guarantee a successful marriage. It will however, show you God's plan for marriage and provide a choice of how you want your marriage to be.

After 24 years of ministry, I have heard and seen a lot, performed countless marriage ceremonies, and counseled individuals and couples. Without any doubt or hesitation, I can tell you that marriage, done right, can be the best decision you ever made in your life. After 14 ½ years, I can say that my marriage has evolved and continues to get better each and every year. That can be your situation as well, but it takes hard work and God at the center of your marriage covenant.

This book will speak to anyone that is seeking and perhaps already living a healthy, happy, and fulfilling marriage. It will also speak to individuals and couples who are "going through hell" in marriage turmoil, and who think that the marriage is over. This book will also speak to individuals who worked hard to create and sustain a marriage, those couples who tried, cried, prayed, obeyed, and still faced despair and ultimately divorce. Whether you are married, single, or hoping to be…There is hope!!! God has promised you a life that is full and one where you can feel hopeful and whole and have great joy in your marriage relationship.

As we walk together through some of the main issues I have found in my years in ministry dealing with marriage, I will show you two sides of relationships and ask that you examine yourself and your relationship to see where you are. In no way will I be able to address every situation you may encounter or have encountered, but at least this is a start for you to examine how to have a marriage that is joyful and pleasing and to give you real ideas on how to handle those life moments in marriage that most go through.

Marriage done God's way can be the greatest institution in the world. If however, you are living in marriage turmoil, with God, your situation can be turned around to become your greatest reward, treasure, and victory (1 Corinthians 15:57)! Whatever your particular situation is, hold tight, this book is for you...

CHAPTER 1

MARRIAGE

1 CORINTHIANS 7:2-3
BUT SINCE THERE IS SO MUCH IMMORALITY, EACH MAN SHOULD
HAVE HIS OWN WIFE, AND EACH WOMAN HER OWN HUSBAND.
THE HUSBAND SHOULD FULFILL HIS MARITAL DUTY TO HIS WIFE,
AND LIKEWISE THE WIFE TO HER HUSBAND.

Why should we even be interested in marriage and writing books about Heaven and Hell in a marriage? When people are "in love" they believe they have all the answers and they don't need to listen to anyone or even look at what God's word says about the institution of marriage. Hopefully this book and some of the information you are about to read will dispel those notions and see that God has a plan for what marriage is supposed to be and the world has distorted that plan and has looked at the marriage bond as being as temporary as the disposable razor they use and then toss into the garbage.

We all have heard the statistics and trends in marriage and divorce, but it seems those are just numbers and we really don't take the time to break those numbers down and really assess what has and is happening in our society. Also, society tells us many lies about how to live and have "happiness" and that is all about us and what makes us happy and the "if it feels good, do it" mentality that we seem to have ingrained in our mores and moral conduct. The media bombards us with couples living together without the marriage commitment and the jumping from bed to bed mentality that shows no value in commitment and monogamous relationships. Why should it surprise us that when our society has strayed so far from what God's plan was that the statistics are what they are? God's word is very clear and why we have strayed so far from it is a question I am sure we need to examine. The Bible says in 1 Corinthians 7:10-11;

> To the married I give this command (not I, but the Lord): A wife must not separate from her husband. But if she does, she must remain unmarried or else be reconciled to her husband. And a husband must not divorce his wife.

How much more plain can God be? If all would simply take the time to read all of 1 Corinthians chapter 7 and take what God has given us, the statistics would perhaps not be what they are and there would not be so many traumas and unhappiness in the relationships and our society would be much better off than it is today.

The following are simply some facts about marriage and the state of marriage in our society today. As you read and contemplate these statistics, I would like you to ask yourself if you see yourself or your marriage in any of the statistics listed. If you do, then you are most likely in the Hell part of marriage rather than the Heaven part. As we go through the rest of the book I ask you do the same thing and look for ways to move your marriage to what God would want rather than what the world would tell you.

The following come from the web site of Dr. Phil (TV Psychologist). The site is www.drphil.com/articles/351. These statistics came from 2003 data so one can only imagine it has continued on the decline even more in the last few years.

- The average age of a woman getting married in the United States is 27.

- The average age of a man getting married in the United States is 29.

- 88 percent of American men and women between the ages of 20 and 29 believe they have a soul mate waiting for them.

- 59 percent of marriages for women under the age of 18 end up in divorce within 15 years. The divorce rate drops to 36 percent for those married at age 20 or older.

- 60 percent of marriages for couples between the ages of 20 and 25 end in divorce.

- 50 percent of all marriages in which the brides are 25 or older result in a failed marriage.

- 65 percent of altar-bound men and women live together before getting married.

- Research indicates that people who live together prior to getting married are more likely to have marriages that end in divorce.

- A recent study on cohabitation concluded that after five to seven years, only 21 percent of unmarried couples were still living together.

- 55 percent of cohabitating couples get married within five years of moving in together. Forty percent of couples who live together break up within that same time period.

- Children of divorce have a higher risk of divorce when they marry, and even higher risk if the person they marry comes from a divorced home. One study found that when the wife alone had experienced a parental divorce, her odds of divorce increased to 59 percent. When both spouses experienced parental divorce, the odds of divorce nearly tripled.

- The likelihood that a woman will eventually marry is significantly lower for those who first had a child out of wedlock. By age 35, only 70 percent of all unwed mothers are married in contrast to 88 percent of women who have not had a child out of wedlock.

Isn't it amazing that we inherently know these facts and we are bombarded with them in the media that we choose to continue down the path to a hellacious marriage rather than a Heavenly one? Even more disturbing, perhaps, are some of the statistics that claim the divorce rate among those who claim to be Christians show no significant difference than those who don't. Some studies even show that the divorce rate in the "Bible Belt" is even higher than other parts of the United States. Of course there could be many reasons for this, but as the world looks at we Christians and judge our actions, how can we justify that we don't heed the words of our Bible and live by them?

To examine the statistics and see what impact a failed marriage can have on the children and the future marriages, how can we not try and find out how to make our marriages work and make them as they were designed to be rather than how the world would tells us it should be? To do this I believe we must look at some of the issues in marriage that come up and cause Christians and non-Christians alike to throw away a marriage and jump from relationship to relationship rather than a committed Godly covenant.

Of course it stands to reason that if a marriage is going to be successful it has to start out on the right path. Finding the person to share your life with is not like going to the store and picking out a new pair of shoes or going to the car dealership and picking out your next car. The problem is in today's society that is exactly the path many take. It never ceases to amaze me how men and women who get married to some person they have picked up in a bar or the internet and have not taken the time to know them, are surprised when the marriage made in Hell comes to an abrupt end. As the shoe shopper looks at the new shoes and imagines how they will look on their feet or the car shopper imagines themselves driving down the road with the wind blowing through their hair and all things right with the world, the marriage shopper does exactly the same thing and romanticizes how their life will be with this new person who looks so good on the outside but they do not take the time to know the inside. I will delve more into this topic in an upcoming chapter.

It is troubling to me that some research comes to the conclusion that those who profess to be Christians have a higher divorce rate than those who don't. Although there are some real concerns about the research, there is really no research that proves the opposite, that Christian divorce rates are lower than those who do not claim to be Christians. We need to get back to the Word of God and follow it to be sure our marriages spend more time from a Heavenly perspective than marriages going through Hell.

In Hebrews 13:4 God tells us that marriage is to be *"held in honor among all..."* The institution of marriage was instituted and ordained by God for the lifelong relationship between one man as husband and one woman as wife. Why has our current society who percentage wise claims to be Christian strayed so far from this directive? At the heart of God's design, marriage is for companionship, intimacy and procreation. God saw in the Garden of Eden the need Adam had for companionship and He created Eve from Adam's rib. Yet, in today's world we see over and over again an attack on the institution of marriage that God designed.

Genesis 2:18, 22, 24 show us God's plan for marriage and the relationship between man and woman. It is such a beautiful and simple story and blueprint for our lives, yet we allow things of the world get in the way and allow our marriages to end in divorce when that is NOT God's plan.

The Lord God said, "It is not good for the man to be alone. I will make a helper suitable for him"...Then the Lord God made a woman from the rib he had taken out of the man, and he brought her to the man.....For this reason a man will leave his father and mother and be united to his wife and they will become one flesh.

What is many times forgotten is how Christ and the disciples used the institution of marriage as an example of Christ's relationship with the church. To see how sacred and meaningful Christ viewed this relationship is reason enough for Christians to take the marriage covenant much more seriously than others. Jesus several times through his ministry from the wedding feast at Cana to the Sermon on the Mount used the institution of marriage to teach the basics about the Kingdom of God.

Examining the statistics of marriage and divorce and simply being an observer of society, it is evident the institution of marriage has been and continues to be under attack. Through the rest of this book it is going to be my intent to show you from a biblical perspective as well as from experiences how to examine marriage from finding your mate to living your life together through Heavenly times as well as times when it seems you are going through Hell for whatever reasons. God says in his word that *"What God has joined together let no man separate"*. How can we attack this trend and overcome issues that cause marriages to end. Yes, I do know there are times when the Bible says divorce is acceptable, but as you study those they are very specific and just because you are tired of being in a marriage from Hell is not enough reason to toss the marriage. For a marriage to be a Heavenly one, it takes work, sacrifice and understanding from both the man and the woman. Let me end this chapter with the idea of *WORK* and give you an acronym to use when you think about this in your marriage.

W = Willing to do what others won't and work at making your marriage a Heavenly one

O = Obey God's word and his direction in what a Heavenly marriage is supposed to be

R = Relate to your spouse and listen to them. Also continue to deepen the relationship

K = Know your husband and wife and their needs and attempt to meet those needs

As you go through the rest of this book and read and learn and examine yourself, if you are married think about the *WORK* it takes to have a Heavenly marriage and if you are not married, think about the *WORK* it is going to take to make sure you are marrying the one God has for you.

APPLICATION AND EXERCISES

1. Think about/discuss marriages that have shown to be successful and stood the test of time. What do you see in the marriage that you believe led to the success?

2. Likewise, think about/discuss marriages that have not worked. What do you see in those marriages that caused them to fail?

3. If you are already married, what did you learn that you can apply to your marriage?

4. If you are not married, how will you use this information to help you find your mate?

5. Do a quick assessment of your family and extended family. How many have been affected by divorce?

6. After reading the statistics, does your family reflect what others are doing or does your family reflect God's plan?

7. What can you do that will show yourself and others that you are serious about a Heavenly marriage? Example: Refuse to watch TV shows that celebrate lifestyles that are counter to God's plan.

8. Take the time to find a couple who have been married for over 25 years and ask if you can sit with them and talk. Ask them specific questions on how their marriage has survived.

9. Find a person(s)who have recently divorced and ask them what finally caused the permanent split. Ask them what they would have done differently.

10. Finally, after having read this chapter, what will you do differently tomorrow than you did today?

CHAPTER 2

YOUR CHOICE, YOUR DESTINY

DEUTERONOMY 30:19-20

"THIS DAY I CALL HEAVEN AND EARTH AS WITNESSES AGAINST YOU THAT I HAVE SET BEFORE YOU LIFE AND DEATH, BLESSINGS AND CURSES. NOW CHOOSE LIFE SO THAT YOU AND YOUR CHILDREN MAY LIVE AND THAT YOU MAY LOVE THE LORD YOUR GOD, LISTEN TO HIS VOICE, AND HOLD FAST TO HIM."

When I read passages of scripture like this one, it becomes very clear to me that the quality of our lives and relationships is directly related to the choices we make in life. One bad relationship decision can cause you to spend all of your emotional energy tolerating a bad marriage and expending negative energy coping with the results of that decision, instead of enjoying the fruit of marriage the way it was intended. Remember that in Deuteronomy 30:19-20, God gave us a multiple choice question. With that question, He also gave us the answers to the question (life vs. death and blessings vs. curses). God tells us which of the two answers to choose (Now choose life) and He also tells us why to choose the right answer (so that your children may live and that you may love the Lord your God, listen to His voice, and hold fast to Him).

The Lord loves us so much that He has provided us with a guide to life in His Word that will direct our paths, protect us from making wrong choices, and to give us the desires of our heart. So why don't we simply make better choices? It's called free will. I often ponder this question during counseling sessions. I usually think, "Well, you had a choice in the beginning my sister or my brother. Why did you choose him or her if you knew you had serious issues from the beginning? God was already showing you the issues you would face, why did you overlook that really important issue?" I often say that couples think they can "beat the odds" or, they really believe that they can change the other person into the person they want them to be. They often think that they are so wonderful and that they will be so great that the other person will miraculously change for them. If he did not have a job when you married him, what would make you think that he was going to become gainfully employed after you got married? If he had three children that he wasn't paying child support for before married you, what would make you think he would take care of your child? If she stayed at the club every weekend hanging out with her friends, what would make you think that she would want to stay home after you married her?

It is so important to simply and honestly acknowledge and accept a person for who he or she [really] is rather than wanting, hoping, or praying that the person is going to be different. A person will only change if he or she has a desire to change. If we were more honest with ourselves in the beginning, it would save a lot of heartache later on. When couples come to me for counseling, I typically begin the session by asking them one question: "Do you want this marriage to work or not?" The answer they give will usually determine the success of the counseling and can often predict the outcome of the marriage. Sometimes couples come to counseling as a last resort. Unfortunately some couples only come to counseling because they are seeking permission, validation, or confirmation of what they already want to do... to get out. Their mind was made up even before they came in. In that case, reconciliation may be impossible if one or both of the individuals are unwilling to listen, to grow, to forgive, to heal the hurts, and resolve their issues. But with God, even the most desperate marriage can be reconciled if both people decide within their hearts to work on the marriage. Whatever you decide to do about your marriage, just know that your thoughts and your actions often predict the outcomes, whether positive or negative.

The late Dr. Edwin Louis Cole wrote in his world renowned book, *Majoring in Men*, that "your life is made up of the choices you made, the words you speak, and the attitude you have." He went on to say, "If you don't like the life you have, change your words and change your choices." This is another way of saying that, *"Death and life are in the power of the tongue and they that love it shall eat the fruit thereof (Proverbs 18:21)."* Many people have made choices that they look back on with regret, wondering how in the world they got where they are. They look back and say, "If

I only knew then what I know now." Unfortunately, there are no "do over's" in this life. But, you can get it right now that you are willing to pay attention and to do things God's way this time.

When it comes to being single and believing God for the "right" mate, faith plays an important role in your decision making. However, faith must accompany Godly wisdom in order to make the right and the best choices for your life. You have to use Godly wisdom so that you will not allow your emotions and feelings to decide for you. Making a decision based on how you feel is not only unwise, but may inevitably cause you to make a permanent decision based on a temporary situation. It is unwise to base permanent decisions on how you feel at any given moment because feelings tend to be very temporary and can change from day to day. You have to give yourself some time to make sure that what you feel is real. Singles may meet a person and "fall in love" after the first date. Well, love at first sight may be real, but you may need to slow things down a bit to be sure that what you feel is consistent over time. Again, don't make a permanent decision about a person because you had a really good date.

Making a wise decision does not mean that you have to become "spooky" with your faith. I would say that a "spooky" Christian is someone that has to pray about every single decision in their life. This person even has to pray about things that God has already given them wisdom about. A "spooky" Christian is someone who does not have the ability to enjoy the simple pleasures of life (having fun socializing with friends or watching a ball game) without thinking those things are too carnal. Spooky Christians make minor decisions huge ones that must be "taken before the Lord" before they can participate in the activity or make a decision. For instance, the Lord has given us good enough sense to know that if it is cold, you need to put a coat on before going outside. He has also given us enough intelligence to be able to decide for ourselves if chicken or fish would be a wise choice for dinner. Now there are many issues to that should be taken to the Lord in prayer. One of those important issues is who to date and ultimately who to marry. God certainly has given us enough Word, wisdom, and sense to know that it is always unwise to date and marry an unsaved person.

Making wise decisions simply means that you must balance faith with the Word of God to ensure that you are making the right choice. In Genesis 2:22, 23, the bible says that God brought Eve to Adam. Then, Adam said that Eve was the bone of my bone and the flesh of my flesh. Adam didn't have to choose Eve although God brought Eve to him. Adam was a free moral agent with the ability to choose. God has given us free will and wants us to be "free" to choose what we believe will make us happy, whole, and fulfilled. God gives us the right to choose what we like. God provided Adam with the selection, but Adam was free to make the final choice. Interestingly enough, Adam did not see any burning bushes, the Red Sea did not part, the stars did not point to Eve, nor did any doves descend upon his shoulder. So, we should not always expect to have any earth-shattering experiences that point us in the right direction. Sometimes God speaks in a quiet, still voice.

Learning to make right, Godly decisions is a matter of:

1. Strengthening your relationship with God;

2. Asking God to lead and guide your choices and ultimately your decisions;

3. Patiently wait to hear from God, trusting that God WILL direct your life;

4. Knowing that God has plans for you that are good and that He wants the best for your life Jeremiah 29:11); and

5. Being obedient once God gives you an answer or directs your heart, even if it's an answer that you do not like or understand at that point.

Trusting God is the "key" to making life altering decisions that have the ability to permanently, positively, or negatively affect your life. You should strive to choose a mate that will help you achieve the great plans that God has for you.

I want to draw attention to the fact that the man is supposed to FIND his wife. Proverbs 18:22 states simply that, "He who finds a wife finds a good thing and finds favor from the Lord..." Ladies, *please* note that this may not be a scriptural mandate, but God wants to clearly give direction on the proper process for dating and relationships. By nature, a man needs to "hunt" and women by nature, need to nurture. If a woman is chasing a man, trying to make or convince him to love her, the relationship simply cannot and will not work according to God's plan. God does not intend for a woman to stalk her intended mate in order to have a relationship with him. The bible does not say that she that "stalketh" a man finds a husband. Even if you "wear him down" and he finally submits to commit, later on, you will grow tired of this one-sided relationship because this is not the way God intends marriage to happen. Sometimes an overly aggressive woman can become less attractive to a "man of character" because it makes him feel that she is overbearing and dominating. In his mind, if she is overbearing and dominating before they get married, he may believe that their relationship will be just like that afterwards. And that kind of relationship is unattractive to a man, regardless of how beautiful the woman is to him.

When I was single, waiting on God to bring me the "right" woman into my life, there were many women that I could have chosen. However, I *truly believed* that God would give me the desires of my heart and I was totally unwilling to compromise on what I believed God wanted for me. There were women who sought my attention or who made themselves known to me. But in my mind, that was the wrong way for me to meet my future wife. There are many relationship books that tell women how to be aggressive and assertive women... that teach them how to "get their man." However, chasing a man to get him to submit to your will can only lead to an unhealthy relationship that will, more often than not, lead to difficulty, heartache, and heartbreak. God provides the options but we must make sure that the choices we make are in harmony with the principles of His Word.

I have been in ministry for 24 years and 18 of those years have been in full-time ministry. It has always amazed me to find that many believers are so balanced in a majority of their lives, yet so unrealistic in the area of choosing a spouse. I have had many men and women tell me, "Pastor, I don't want anyone that has children." Yet, they have several. I have had people tell me that they want a man that is "saved, with a good job, and makes a lot of money," yet they themselves have bad credit, no savings, and a stack of unpaid or poorly paid bills. Men have told me that they want a woman that is a size 2, yet when you look at them, they are no walking trophies themselves. The point I am trying to make is that we all have an idea of what and who we want, but it is important to make sure that we are not setting ourselves up for disappointment by having *unrealistic expectations*. Let me say that again, "You will be disappointed if you set yourself up with unrealistic expectations." Your Boaz may not come riding in on a white horse ready to steal you away from your job, bills, and troubles. Stop watching Lifetime movies and start listening to the Holy Spirit. Yes, God has the ability to give you the desires of your heart, but it is also important to realize that, in fairness to everyone involved, *you must work to become what you desire.*

Let me continue to expound upon the term, "unrealistic expectations!" An example of an unrealistic expectation is to expect something from another person that you are unwilling or unable to give yourself. For example, if you are an unhappy person or a person that has low self-confidence, you should not look for a person to make you happy or to make you feel better about yourself. Happiness and self-confidence come from within. If you are waiting for someone to make you happy in order to be happy, the other person will never be able to fulfill that desire for you for any extended period of time. Having that expectation is like trying to fill a bucket with a hole in it. The more the person fills the bucket, the more is required to fill it. If you are that bucket with the hole in it, over time, your mate will get tired of trying to fill the bucket because it will never be filled. This may be a too simple of an example, but there rings some truth to it. Having realistic expectations is an acknowledgment that not one of us is perfect but we should seek to compliment each other rather than attempt to become *whole* as a result of being with another person. Expecting another person to "make you whole" is an unrealistic, unhealthy, and unreasonable expectation that no one could possibly live up to over time. I joke in sermons that some singles would have turned down Jesus because He had on dusty sandals and wore a shaggy beard. Would you have turned Jesus down because he didn't look the part of the "perfect" man?

During my junior year of college, God called me into the ministry. Within a year, I was teaching Bible studies on campus and preaching from time to time on Sunday mornings in areas churches. I found that temptation does not stop because you accept Christ as your Lord and Savior. Temptation did not stop because God called me into ministry. In fact, the opposite may have been true because I am convinced that the enemy was angry that I answered the Lord's Call with such fervor and conviction. The temptation intensified as I became more assured and more committed to follow the path that I knew God has placed me on. But, I had to make some serious decisions at that time. I knew that if I was going to be successful at living the life Christ had planned for me, I would *have to* fortify my faith. Make no mistake about it, this was not an easy life to live. I was a young man determined to live "right" while living life as a student, an athlete, and while being pursued by women who knew me as such. It was not easy, but with God, IT WAS POSSIBLE TO OVERCOME TEMPTATION. In God's word, 1 Corinthians 10:13 tells us that there is no temptation that is uncommon to man and that God is faithful and will always provide a way out if we choose to, and really want to get out of any compromising situation. But you also have to know that God will not override your choice to sin.

You must make a decision to live "right" and to remain celibate. When I say celibate, that includes activity such as foreplay, masturbation, and phone sex, just to name a few. Yes, even those things are included in living a celibate lifestyle. The greatest temptation you must face is the decision to protect yourself from yourself. Nobody knew me better than I knew myself, so I had to make decisions that would not compromise my integrity or God's plans for my life. What I mean by this is that I had to make sure that I did not put myself in situations where sin was easily accessible to me or that would cause me too much temptation. The first step in making the right decision was to be absolutely certain that *I truly desired to be in God's Will.*

In my study, I came across a scripture that I had heard so many times as a church benediction. That scripture from Jude 24 read, "Now unto to Him who is able to keep you from falling..." This scripture was truly a revelation to me. This scripture that many preachers used to close the Order of Service became a way of life to me. I used this scripture to live my daily walk. I realized that God was (and is) able to keep me, but "the catch" was that I had to want to be kept. The same holds true for you. God is able to keep you from falling if you are determined to avoid falling. Before long [during that time], I looked up and realized that it had been a year and God was still keeping me. I had not fallen prey to the tricks and attacks of the enemy. Now, this may not seem like much to some of you, but for me, a then 20 year old athlete on a college campus with many temptations, it was a huge achievement and accomplishment. God was teaching me how to live for Him. He was teaching me lessons that I had to learn in order to be where He is continuing to take me today. Then next thing I knew, it had been two years, then three years, and eventually I graduated from college and started my first teaching job, preaching on weekends, and God was still keeping me. Several years later, God called me to move to Indianapolis and start my first church. I was a single man, serving God as a Pastor, but God was still keeping me.

After eight years of experiencing God's Keeping Power, I met my future wife. One of the things that motivated me most about meeting, knowing, dating, and ultimately believing God for my wife, was that I had an incredible and blessed testimony to share with her about my wait and God's "keeping" Power. Having that knowledge and her trust that I would not compromise my integrity or hers enabled us to build a relationship that had a foundation grounded in Godly Principles. You should know that in marriage, trust is everything. Making a decision, the right decision, can lead you into a relationship that is holy and acceptable to you, your spouse, and to God.

"I would like you to be free from concern. An unmarried man is concerned about the Lord's affairs- how he can please the Lord. But a married man is concerned about the affairs of the world-how he can please his wife- and his interests are divided." (1 Corinthians 7:32-3)

This scripture leads me to conclude that God's will for the believer is undivided interests. It certainly isn't that you don't have a life outside of church and ministry because it is important that we all live a balanced life. However, Paul is saying that the single years can be some of the most effective years of your life in getting involved in the things of God (choir, youth ministry, etc.). Single people must take advantage of that particular season of singleness and do as much for the Kingdom as possible. There will come a time when the single person's concern will change to that of their marriage and their spouse—as it should. The married person will have to, by necessity and design, divide their time between family and ministry. The key to a successful life in marriage and ministry is to have your ministry and family interests and priorities in line.

In choosing a spouse, God does not bring people together by common interests but by common purpose. Before you get emotionally involved with anyone, you must take an honest look at the person. You must ask them several important questions about what they believe. Additionally, you must watch to see if their actions support their words. That is, don't worry as much about what they say as you observe what they do. Ask the following questions of yourself as well as the person:

1. What do you believe God has called you to do?
2. Does this person's purpose "fit" into the context of what God is calling you to do?
3. Do their actions "line up with" what they say they believe about God?

This is where things get sticky for many people. Usually you have already met someone that you are physically attracted to, you have already begun spending time together, and your feelings are already developing. Along the way, perhaps you are seeing things that make you question their sincerity, their devotion to the things of God, and you may even begin to question their salvation. But, your feelings are already involved and it is too difficult to walk away at this point. This is why it is important to ask these important questions up front before you get your feelings invested. After the feelings and the emotional attachments get too strong, many people go into denial, hoping the person will change, or hoping that they can change the person. Perhaps you are lonely and simply thankful to have someone special in your life after having a relationship drought. But, it is critical to allow your wisdom to "kick in" so that you won't have to expend that emotional and often negative energy tolerating a bad relationship and ultimately a bad marriage.

One of the most important ways to overcome loneliness and depression as a single is by remaining active. The enemy wants to use your loneliness to make you fall into various forms of temptation. Never put your life on hold while you are "believing God" for a relationship, whether you are male or female. When that person finally comes into your life, you want to be so busy being productive that he or she becomes a part of your life, not your reason for existing.

When you change your life to fit someone else's life or make them the center of your world, they have become your god. When you allow a person to become your reason for living, it becomes too much pressure for them and it is possible that you end up making them your god-taking your attention off of the things of God. You must ask yourself if you are allowing that person to draw you from God and/or the things of God (daily devotional time, personal study time, attending bible study, participating in ministry opportunities, attending worship services). You should also honestly ask yourself if you are allowing that new person to change your focus and your reason for existing. Have you begun taking time away from your ordinary responsibilities and activities you enjoyed previously in order to spend time, perhaps unhealthy amounts of time with that new person? You must be honest and open with yourself. If you find that you are guilty of making that person the center of your life, it is inherent that you redefine the relationship yourself and reprioritize your life with God as the Head of your life.

12 Or else, if indeed you do go back, and cling to the remnant of these nations—these that remain among you—and make marriages with them, and go in to them and they to you, 13 know for certain that the LORD your God will no longer drive out these nations from before you. But they shall be snares and traps to you, and scourges on your sides and thorns in your eyes, until you perish from this good land which the LORD your God has given you. Joshua 23: 12-13 (NKJV)

Scripture tells us in 2 Corinthians 6 to not be unequally yoked with unbelievers. In order to have a deeper understanding, it is important to define yoke. A yoke is a type of harness which connects a pair of animals together to plow a field. When Paul makes the statement, it is important to know that it is a symbol of burden or oppression from your responsibilities…a burden you have to bear in order to take care of your responsibilities.

In Matthew 11: Jesus said, "Take my yoke…for my burden is easy and my burden is light. You never saw a horse yoked together with a mule. The nature of a horse is different than that of a mule because if you yoke them together, they will pull in different directions. Make no mistake; the wrong relationships will pull you (and your life) in the wrong direction. However, using the same example, if a yoke ties two animals together, then when you are yoked in the right relationship, heading in the same direction, it should make your life easier not more difficult.

It is amazing to me that people in love or with the idea of being in love, always think they can beat the odds of being successful in the wrong relationship. We must remember that when we are told to not be unequally yoked with unbelievers, it is a mandate more than just sound advice. It never fails, even among believers, that there is always someone who knows the truth about their relationship, but somehow deceive themselves into believing that they can beat the odds-that their relationship will work out despite all the evidence to the contrary. A woman may tell herself, "I know he isn't saved but if I get with him, I can change him." It is hard enough to change your own bad habits and actions, so what makes you think that your witness is going to be so profound that you can change another adult person's behavior? It rarely happens. In fact, typically in trying to change another person, you will end up frustrating yourself and the other person too. People generally change only when they have a mind to change themselves. It is not worth the effort to try. You may end up losing more than the hope of changing someone. You may end up losing the person as well as yourself, and your God-given identity in the process.

Being in an unauthorized relationship may mean more than a believer marrying an unbeliever. Being in an unauthorized relationship may also mean any of the following:

1. Both spouses may be believers but have different levels of spiritual maturity. They may act and respond to similar actions in different ways;

2. Spouses may have different goals and ambitions in ministry. They may have a different call to Kingdom work.

3. Becoming involved with a person that God has specifically warned you against.

4. Becoming emotionally involved with a coworker or anyone of the opposite sex that is not your spouse. For example, if you are having recurrent conversations, text messaging, or thoughts of anyone that is not

your spouse or that your spouse cannot or does not know about, you may be involved in an emotional affair. End it right away!

5. All of your spiritual strength will go into making the relationship work, trying to save your spouse or trying to survive a relationship that is spiritually, physically, or emotionally unhealthy or unrewarding;

6. The wrong relationship will move you out of your place of purpose and dislodge you from your destiny;

7. The wrong relationship will change your personality; you may start acting like that person rather than the person that God created you to be. Remember that bad company corrupts good character.

You have become "off track" when you are in **any** wrong relationship. In these cases, the enemy will go after your heart because you are controlled by your emotions. If the enemy can control your emotions, he can control you psychologically and ultimately, physically. Relationship decisions should be made that are based on character and character development. Strive to live a life that gives testimony to your love of God!

APPLICATION AND EXERCISES

1. Review the scriptures where God shows us how to choose our spouse. If you are single, how does this speak to you? If you are married, are you equally yoked and if not what can you and should you do?

2. If you are single, what are you doing to be sure God is "still keeping you" as you wait for His direction in a marriage partner?

3. If you are married, what are you doing to be sure your marriage is continually being a Heavenly one rather than going through Hell?

4. If you seem to be going through Hell in a relationship, whether married or single, what is causing that situation?

5. Find a married couple that seems to have a Heavenly marriage. Sit with them and talk about how they found one another and how they knew God was in the decision to marry.

6. Search the scriptures and see if God speaks to a marriage that has one spouse being a believer and the other not. If you do find it, what does He say about the relationship?

CHAPTER 3

UNTIL DEBT DO US PART

LUKE 14:28-30

SUPPOSE ONE OF YOU WANTS TO BUILD A TOWER. WILL HE
NOT FIRST SIT DOWN AND ESTIMATE THE COST TO SEE IF HE
HAS ENOUGH MONEY TO COMPLETE IT? FOR IF HE LAYS THE
FOUNDATION AND IS NOT ABLE TO FINISH IT, EVERYONE WHO SEES
IT WILL RIDICULE HIM, SAYING, 'THIS FELLOW BEGAN TO BUILD
AND WAS NOT ABLE TO FINISH.

It is important to deal with the subject of finances because so many couples find themselves headed to divorce court because of problems with financial mismanagement and overwhelming debt. It is important to understand that family stability is difficult to achieve when couples do not have financial stability. As a result, money issues become so large that it becomes the major irritant between couples. It is sad and unfortunate that couples allow money to divide what God has brought together.

Prior to getting married, couples should have honest discussions about finances and debt. In addition to having discussions about finances, couples should also develop a spending and savings plan. It is important to know your intended spouse's credit history, amount of debt and savings they have, any child support and/or alimony payments, etc. It is important to have this information prior to the commitment of marriage because you may decide that you simply cannot afford to get married. It may sound strange or seem unkind to say, but sometimes couples simply can't afford to get married. Unfortunately some married couples, because of their financial instability and debt, can't afford to get divorced. These reasons suggest that early and regular discussions about money and implementing strong strategies within the marriage have the potential of easing financial burdens and hardships. Financial stability will *not* happen unless and until both partners agree and implement strong principles and commit themselves to follow an orderly and sensible plan to live a life that is pleasing to God. Planning for the life you want to have is essential for marital success. My spiritual father, Bishop I. V. Hilliard, says that, "You are going to have to live in your future. So, you might as well live in one that you plan for." There are so many scriptures that guide our financial stewardship. God has provided so many wonderful scriptures that gives hope and help for framing our thinking, actions, and plans for marriage:

I am firmly convinced that you must have these open and honest conversations before marriage because you should not marry anyone that you don't trust or that you cannot talk with honestly about money. You must understand that your marriage cannot go to the next level until you are transparent about everything. In Genesis 2, the bible shows us how God brought everything together and in Chapter 3, the enemy takes it apart. One thing we find is that when God brought Adam and Eve together, they were naked and not ashamed. There was nothing between them to hide behind; they were completely exposed yet, they were not ashamed of their condition in any way. Like Adam and Eve before the fall, there should be nothing in your life or the life of your spouse that should be hidden from the other. That type of transparency is one that God can do something with.

Parents must educate their children as early as possible about issues related to proper money management so that they begin to study and implement the principles as individuals before joining in marriage with another individual who may also have limited understanding about finances. Love our children enough so that we set the financial stage for generations to come. The bible says that a wise father leaves an inheritance for his children's children (Proverbs 13:22). The children need to be able to build on a strong foundation so that there is generational wealth for years to come.

There are many reasons that couples find themselves heavily in debt, not knowing how to release themselves from the heavy burden. For some, the dismal state of their finances is due to:

1. Lack of knowledge: not having a foundation or real understanding of money management

2. Selfishness, self-reliant will: refusing to obey or submit to God's principles of stewardship. Scripture warns us in Proverbs 13:18 that, "He who ignores

discipline comes to poverty and shame, but whoever heeds correction is honored."

3. Impatience: making impetuous decisions that lead to overspending and an unwillingness to wait

Below is a list of specific, real-life and examples of spending mistakes made in families that I have counseled. This is by no means an exhaustive list, but I want to give you examples so you can avoid making some of these very common mistakes.

Spending that has the potential of causing marital stress:

1. Buying houses that they are not able to afford: monthly payments, upkeep, furniture, insurance, home improvements, insurance, taxes...

2. Buying cars that they cannot afford: monthly payments, upkeep, maintenance, insurance tags, taxes

3. Trying to impress the Joneses'

4. Living above their means - not planning and spending wisely based on current income

5. Trying to live as well as if not better than their parents too quickly

6. Buying too many clothes. You know you have too many clothes if you don't have as much money saved as you have clothing value

7. Buying too much jewelry (excessive, expensive purchases)

8. Wasted opportunities to advance themselves professionally or academically

9. Renting rather than purchasing a home or other real estate

10. Making the children idols by buying them everything they want:
    a. Not teaching them proper financial stewardship
    b. Huge holidays and birthdays that the family cannot afford

11. Expensive, unaffordable vacations

12. Paying for household items with credit rather than paying cash

13. Unnecessary luxuries and purchases
    a. Grass cutting, landscaping
    b. Maid service
    c. Laundering services, including dry cleaning

14. Excessive grooming services that are unaffordable
    a. Hair
    b. Nails

15. Pet Ownership
    a. Grooming
    b. Feeding
    c. Well visits and sick visits

16. Financing family dysfunction- Providing loans and gifts to family and friends

17. Not having a savings plan, financial plan, or financial advisor

18. Emotional shopping (shopping when bored, happy or sad)

19. Not being educated in the area of finances and making
    impulsive, uneducated decisions

    Through wisdom a house is built, and by
    understanding it is established; and by
    knowledge the rooms shall be filled with all
    precious and pleasant riches. (Proverbs 24:3-4)

    May he grant you your heart's desire and fulfill
    all your plans! (Psalm 20:4)

In order to change our thinking about money, we
must come to a very basic fact. Some of us have limited
understanding about money because our parents had limited
understanding. As a result, our financial strategy was to do
what our parents did; go to work, pay bills, provide for the
family, and love each other the best way that we can. While
going to work, paying bills, and living a day-to-day life are
all admirable actions, many learned to survive living from
paycheck to paycheck. I have a personal responsibility to
release information to empower and enable you to break the
spirit of lack, to take authority over paycheck to paycheck
living, and to watch your families go to new levels.

Couples should learn early in their marriage that the
marriage should be evolving all the time, never growing
static or boring. The marriage, as well as each individual
should be growing and developing from one level to the
next. Many people are resistant to change and although
their current living is uncomfortable, they are unable or
unwilling to do what is necessary to produce necessary
change in their lives and in their marriage. It has been said
that change is not a destination, but a process that we must

constantly be involved in. The bible says that we are being changed from glory to glory in God's image (II Corinthians 3:18). So, in order to change the divorce statistics, we must change our thinking about finances and ultimately break old, destructive patterns that lead us to marital breakup. We must understand that God is concerned about every area of our lives, including how we use, spend, and invest the resources that He has provided for us.

Can you imagine getting your next paycheck and being in a position where you can provide for your family, save, invest, tithe, and still have money left over for all your needs and many of your wants? My goal is to help you to move into the position that God wants us all to be in with regard to our finances.

Nothing can kill a marriage faster than the bondage of financial mismanagement and marital debt. Often, believers think of bondage as it relates to the typical sins of adultery, lying, stealing, killing, and fornication. While all of these acts are sinful, be reminded that anything that falls short of God's glory or His plan for our lives may be sinful. So many well intended Christians who love the Lord often miss the mark in the area of finances, thereby literally "killing their marriages." Only when we become exhausted enough about our financial situations and repulsed by our lack of financial intelligence and the bondages we create by our actions, will we become better stewards of the resources that God has given us.

Luke 14:28 tells us that thought and planning should go into every financial purchase that we make. We should consider the purchase and consider the financial, physical, emotional, and spiritual costs of making a purchase or investment. Overextending yourself financially may cause as much emotional stress as it does financial stress. Likewise, we know that our bodies are made up of a triune that consists of the mind, the body, and the spirit. When one area is out of order, the others suffer as well. And, if you don't feel well emotionally, it has the potential to extend over into your physical or spiritual health and so on.

The objective of financial stewardship and financial management is to make wise purchases. You must ask yourself one important question, "Is this purchase a need or a want?" A need is something that you must have in order to survive. Needs are classified as food, clothing, and shelter. Wants are those things that you desire to have but do not actually need. Wants are those things that are backed up by your ability to spend more time, energy, and money to have. God wants to give us the desires of our heart. So, if you sacrifice now, you can have options later.

When considering whether an item is a need or want, there has to be a healthy combination of the two in order for family members to feel that they are living a life that is happy, fulfilling, fun, and wholesome. There is a difference between being a good steward of your finances and being cheap. Sometimes people hold on to their money so tight and justify doing so. My wife and I have been on a budget from day one of our marriage. She allowed me to be the steward of our household income. It was never my money and her money, it has always been "our money". Before any major purchase is made we discuss it and agree on an amount we will spend. We didn't have much to work with early on in our marriage, but even as our net worth has increased we still practice the principle of communication and agreement before any major commitment of our resources. What we always live by, however, is that we give to God before we take for ourselves and tithing is an integral part of our financial planning. In my book <u>**Smart Money Management**</u> I go into the biblical basis for this important part of any marriage.

With the current state of our economy, showing wisdom is extremely important. In some cases, one or both individual is walking in fear of not having enough. Walking in fear means that they hold onto everything they have for fear that something may happen that would devastate the family. God did *not* give us a spirit of fear. When fear is the motivating factor in our decisions, it may cause us to go to extremes in trying to take care of our families. In this case, they may justify their position by saying it's stewardship when in reality it's fear shaping the thinking and ultimately, the actions. There is something to be said for being careful and using wisdom in our economy, but we must be sure that our concerns are not making our family members miserable and unable to live up to one-sided expectations.

When you are considering a purchase, it is necessary to consider the cost (Luke 14:28) prior to making the purchase. It is important to be able to afford whatever you need or want to purchase with ease. High ticket items are houses, cars, appliances, furniture, etc. However, careful planning should also be made for smaller, less expensive items as well. Whether the item is an expensive or less expensive item, there are several basic rules to follow prior to purchasing any item.

1. **Is this item really needed?** Individuals must determine whether this item is really needed. They should decide whether this purchase is an impulse or emotional purchase that would translate into being a strong want rather than a need. Further, individuals must ask themselves if they can live without the desired item. If it is decided that the individual or the family can live without the item, then they must decide to delay or cancel the purchase.

2. **Set and follow a family budget.** Have a monthly spending plan (budget) that will help the family stay within a comfortable range of living. After reviewing and implementing the budget, you should carefully consider whether the family can afford the purchase. A budget will tell you where your priorities are, where money is being spent, and whether money is "falling between the cracks." When considering a family budget, the family must create a budget that allows them to live a balanced family life. If the budget does not meet the needs and wants of each member, it will be difficult to follow and maintain the budget.

3. **Comparison shop.** If it has been decided that a purchase is needed, then couples should do their homework before making the purchase. Individuals should check the price and quality of the item at different stores so they can determine the best available item for their budget. You should also consider reviewing sales papers, television advertising, resource books, and also use the internet to comparison shop for intended items.

4. **Avoid overuse or misuse of credit cards.** Pay cash for

items to avoid the overuse or misuse of credit cards. And, ask yourself if you really need the item now. You must consider the short-term and long-term costs of making this purchase now. If you have to use credit in order to secure the purchase, what will be the interest rate and estimated final cost of that purchase? Will you only be able to afford the minimum monthly payment which will increase the overall cost of the item? Please remember that banks make their money from the interest charged rather than for the actual cost of the item. After you have considered the full cost, ask yourself again if you can afford the purchase.

5. **Get financial assistance!** Sometimes couples wait too long or are too embarrassed about their financial situation to seek help in the form of assistance, available resources, or advice. Please do not be embarrassed to ask for help or to seek help before it is too late. Seek the advice of an accountant, a financial planner, or credit counselor that may have the ability to assist you with your financial plans or help you get your financial situation straightened out. There are free, non-profit, and government programs that you may be able to take advantage of before considering for-profit agencies that you may not be able to afford. If you begin having financial problems, do not ignore the problem. Call the creditor and explain your situation. They may have repayment or modification plans that you may be able to take advantage of. Remember, delaying the addressing of a problem or ignoring the problem will not make it go away.

6. So, how do we keep our marriages from being strapped financially and live a marriage in a more Heavenly manner? I am sure I don't have all the answers, but as I said before, my goal is to at least give you some things to think about when preparing to marry or living in a Godly marriage that is stable financially.

1. **Make more money**
   a. Avoid procrastinating, fear, or laziness in the area of improving your ability to gain additional wealth. Scripture tells us that he becomes poor who works with a lazy hand, but the hand of the diligent brings wealth. (Proverbs 10:4 NIV)
   b. Apply for higher paying positions within or outside your current employer
   c. Get additional training or licensures
   d. Go back to school for advanced degrees or certifications
   e. Start a small business

2. **Learn how to protect your money**
   a. Wills – set up a will and tell your family where your will is. A regular will dictates what will happen to your estate, your property, and your guardians or children after your death or if you become unable to care for yourself.
   b. Trusts – a legal process that keeps your possessions out of probate court and you can transfer your property, assets, your property, assets, bank accounts, real estate, to a person or persons you "trust" while you are alive.

c. Life Insurance – families should have at minimum, Term Life insurance. An important rule of thumb about life insurance is to set up a policy so that your family would not miss your income or have to lower their standard of living for a specific period of time if a spouse should pass away.

d. Savings – have at least three (3) months of salary saved for emergencies.

3. **Leveraging your money** – using your money to make money. The earlier an individual decides to invest, the more earning potential they have with that investment. Early investments are wise to produce the greatest and most effective long-term results. If a young adult invests in a simple I.R.A. by age 21, in 20-30 years, that ROI (Return on Investment) has the potential of netting them a million plus dollars toward retirement by the time that investor reaches 65 years of age.

a. **Make wise investment decisions.** Never invest in things you don't understand. Educate yourself in a particular area of investing that interests you. Take courses, join investment clubs, etc.

b. **Invest in Real Estate** – God's promise to Israel was real estate. Not only did God deliver them from an oppressive situation, but He also gave them real estate. No one can take what you own and control by your ownership. God's promise for us was not for us to rent. When we rent, we make someone else rich. When we own property, we make ourselves rich. Couples should take advantage of first time home ownership programs offered by federal and state agencies. They should consider Federal Housing Administration (FHA) financing options made available to first time home owners.

c. The bible tells us to **be the lender and not the borrower.** In our time, we can finance anything (from a microwave to furniture). But our objective should be to earn interest on investments.

d. Always consider the **current inflation rate** is 2.72% (based on data released January 15, 2009 for December 2009). The inflation rate is the rate by which prices increase or decrease within a specified period of time. It is likely that next year we will pay a higher price for an item than we paid for the same item at the same time of the year. When we save or invest, we must make sure that the investments outperform the price of inflation. Otherwise, we are gradually working our way back to a place where we are constantly struggling.

e. We must **make sure that our retirement accounts are a good investment.** Many of us have no idea what type of retirement account(s) we have on our job. Many of us don't know what types of stocks are within our accounts. The key to financial success is starting early with proper planning.

A common practice that many adults can no longer afford to make is the expectation that they can depend on Social Security benefits to provide for or supplement their retirement income. For many people under 40 years of age, it is highly likely that the Social Security fund that our parents and grandparents depended on for support, may be deficient, defunct or deplete by the time they reach retirement age, if not before. And, even if it does exist in part, it may not be enough to provide individuals the quality of life that they need or expect to have.

In order to create a plan that will increase your financial solvency, you must decide and fully commit to reduce or eliminate your debt. Even after the decision has been made, it is imperative to create a debt reduction plan, a spending plan/budget, and most important, prepare to fully implement the plans for maximum benefit to change and improve your financial future. Romans 13:8 tells us to "let no debt remain outstanding, except the continuining debt to love one another, for he who loves his fellowman has fulfilled the law." As a child of God, it is your responsibility to God and to your creditors to pay the bills you have created.

Again, I do not have all the answers, but here are a few specific ways a family may look to reduce and/or eliminate debt from their lives. To have a marriage that continues to be Heavenly rather than one that causes the family Hell, reducing or eliminating debt is a way to achieve that goal.

1. *Create a debt reduction plan.*
   a. Commit to repaying all of your debt in the most timely and responsible way possible. Having commitment and self control, the ability to be in

control of yourself so as to be in harmony with God's Will, to use restraint particularly when you have the ability to purchase items you want but you decide not to.

b. The general rule in a debt reduction plan is to pay the highest interest rate debt first to eliminate the one(s) costing you the most money.

c. Pay extra money on your lowest bills to rid yourself of those smaller accounts. When one is paid off, use that money to increase the payments on the next one and so on.

2. *Make at least one extra payment on your mortgage every year.* You can cut years off your mortgage using this debt payoff strategy. You can work with your mortgage company to make biweekly payments of your mortgage. By working with your lender, you have the opportunity to decrease your interest applied to the loan by the bank. Additionally, you could achieve the same goal by making your regular monthly payments and writing an extra check at the end of the year.

3. *Use your income tax refund to pay down debts.* If your average annual income tax refund is $2000, you should consider paying a portion to reduce your debt and then to increase your savings with the remaining portion.

4. *Transfer your credit card debt to a new credit card that gives you 0% interest for one year.* This strategy

will afford you the opportunity to have 12 months of interest-free payments that go directly to the principal of that particular loan. This will also enable you to reduce or eliminate a particular debt quickly.

5. *Downsize.* Determine if there are areas in your life where downsizing may be an appropriate action to help the family reach its financial goals. You may need to downsize your home, car, or perhaps allow the children to enroll in public schools vs. expensive private schools. If it is decided that downsizing may be necessary, do not wait. Use wisdom and gain advice from trusted counselors.

Rapid debt reduction plans include plans for lowering and reducing debt quickly. These plans require a hefty sacrifice and total commitment. When you are committed to eliminating your debt and managing your finances in ways that are pleasing to God, He will work toward accelerating your program and bring you out of debt miraculously.

Many who are reading this book may think I am crazy talking about all these things when they are worrying about how to put food on the table let alone trying to reduce or eliminate debt. That is exactly the kind of mind set that I feel needs to be abolished. If we have a scarcity mentality then our resources will surely be scarce. We need to have an abundance mentality and expect and work toward that rather than being satisfied with our present state. One of the ways we can do this is to begin in earnest establishing a savings account.

The first step in developing a savings plan is to identify your family's goals for your savings. The savings plan is developed with your family monthly budget in mind. It is important to reevaluate the plan from time to time to determine if adjustments need to be made to the plan. The family may decide to develop the following:

1. Household Savings Account

2. Vacation Savings Account-money intended for family vacation needs

3. Emergency Savings Account-money needed for unexpected expenses such as a water heater, new tires, appliance that breaks down, etc.

4. Christmas Savings Account-money set aside for Christmas presents or holiday expenses.

5. Education Fund-money regularly set aside for children's college expenses.

A typical household budget is one that includes all expenses that the family has on a monthly basis. One of my earlier books, **_Smart Money Management_**, goes into great detail on how to set up and live a productive, Godly life when it comes to money. Without realizing the importance of finances and the effects they have on a relationship, the marriage will most likely become one of the statistics stated earlier or at least the marriage will be going through Hell rather than being a Heavenly one.

APPLICATION AND EXERCISES

1. Do you have a family budget? If not, why not? If not, take the time to look at **_Smart Money Management_** and establish a beginning budget.

2. Take the time to talk with a financial planner and look at your future for;
   a. Retirement
   b. Educational needs
   c. Automobiles
   d. Leaving a legacy for your family

3. Review your insurance policies and be sure you are adequately covered.

4. Examine God's word and find at least two scriptures that speak to finances and living with His plan.

5. Carefully examine your cash flow and be sure you "pay yourself" each pay to be sure to plan for the future.

6. Find a younger married couple that appears to be financially stable. Sit with them and find out what they have done to put themselves into their present state.

7. Identify a retired couple who seem to have an abundance life style. Sit with them and have them give you five things they did so they could be in the position they are in.

8. After completing 6 and 7 above, how will you use this information to change your own financial future?

CHAPTER 4

HOW TO LOVE

EPHESIANS 5:22-27

WIVES, SUBMIT TO YOUR HUSBANDS AS TO THE LORD. FOR THE
HUSBAND IS THE HEAD OF THE WIFE AS CHRIST IS THE HEAD OF
THE CHURCH, HIS BODY, OF WHICH HE IS THE SAVIOR. NOW AS THE
CHURCH SUBMITS TO CHRIST, SO ALSO WIVES SHOULD SUBMIT TO
THEIR HUSBANDS IN EVERYTHING.
HUSBANDS, LOVE YOUR WIVES, JUST AS CHRIST LOVED THE CHURCH
AND GAVE HIMSELF UP FOR HER TO MAKE HER HOLY, CLEANSING HER
BY THE WASHING WITH WATER THROUGH THE WORD, AND TO PRESENT
HER TO HIMSELF AS A RADIANT CHURCH, WITHOUT STAIN OR WRINKLE
OR ANY OTHER BLEMISH, BUT HOLY AND BLAMELESS.

As husbands it is important that you understand that whatever goes on in your house, even when it is not your fault, it still your responsibility. One of the problems in our society today is that too many people want to be married but function like they are single. Many men fail to understand that until you make your woman a priority, the marriage will never get to where you want it to be and where God designed it to be. Likewise, women fail to follow the scripture and want to dominate the household and their husband and don't want to submit to the authority of God and the authority of the husband in the home. I suggest to you that it is time for men and women to get delivered from this "Play Station" mentality and get serious about turning our marriages and families around to become what God designed them to be.

Proverbs 18:22 says *"he that finds a wife finds a good thing, and obtains favor from the Lord"*. This is powerful because the text is suggesting that the benefit of God approving your selection is the fact that He confirms his approval with favor! What that means to me is that finding that mate that God has intended for both the husband and wife will bring great favor from God and therefore happiness and joy. Not to say, once again, that there won't be times of your marriage going through Hell, but with God's favor, how can you fail?

In every relationship it is critical that you learn to identify the needs of your mate and put yourself in a position where you are more than able to meet those needs. But at the same time it is also critical that each party understand what needs are supposed to be met by the spouse and what are supposed to be met by God. I say this because if you don't learn how to differentiate between the two you will put pressure on your husband or wife to fulfill needs that only God is capable of meeting. An example of this would be self esteem. Don't think you can make your spouse responsible for your own self esteem. That is a need only God can meet. When you understand, through prayer and study of the scriptures, how God values you as a person, it frees you from the pressure to be anything but yourself and frees you from the thoughts that it is your husband or wife's responsibility to stroke your ego.

In Genesis 3:16 God said to the woman: *"your desire shall be for your husband, and he shall rule over you"*. A woman has two primary concerns; the family and security. Because she was made from the rib of man her primary needs are met through a close relationship with her spouse. Because the woman was made from the rib of man there is a completeness she feels when she and her husband are connected and the relationship is secure. It stands to reason when the woman does not feel loved and connected that the marriage will not be what God intended. Likewise, when the man feels unloved and unconnected with his wife the same tragic results can occur.

Knowing that the marriage needs the feeling of security and love, isn't it understandable that it is hard for a woman to respect a man that says he loves her, but does not provide for her? How can a husband expect a wife to submit to what she cannot respect? I am not saying here that all wants of either party are that important, but meeting the wife and family needs is the responsibility of the husband and he cannot expect the family to respect him if he does not meet the needs of the family and provide a safe and nurturing environment for them. It is hard, especially in these economic times to adequately provide for a family, but in God's plan it is the husband's responsibility.

I may anger some with this next statement, but I tell you it is my belief that it was not God's original design for the woman to have to work outside the home. My wife is a career woman so I have nothing against every woman doing whatever they were gifted to do, but my point is I believe that one of the reasons why so many marriages and families are functioning in the way they are or not functioning at all and ending in divorce is that stress and constant pressure has become the norm because we have stepped outside of God's original design. We concentrate more on things of this world than things of the next and our wants overcome our desire for a Godly marriage and family.

Some of you may be angry with me at this point and don't think I understand that you can't afford for the wife to be at home. My response to that is to ask yourself the question of whether or not you have or desire so much "stuff" that it takes two incomes to sustain your family. The answer to this dilemma is that if it is the desire of the wife that she be at home or that your marriage seems to be in Hell because of the stress of financial burdens or lack of time to care for and love each other, then you need to fix it! You need to position your family to a financial position so that you can function without your wife's salary. Please take the time to digest this before you throw out my thoughts. Even if your wife wants to work and have a career, think about how much less stress your family would have if you lived your daily lives as if she were not working and the money she brought in was not imperative to "paying the bills". I again state my original belief that God's design is for the wife to be at home to nurture the family, but if she desires to work, it should be because both the husband and wife want her to and is a want to, not a need to.

What can easily happen in a marriage is that husbands

and wives can easily forget to love one another and provide for their needs because they get so caught up in what they do rather than who they are and who they are supposed to be in God's eyes. The world tells us that we have to constantly climb the ladder of success and things and wants are more important than our relationships with one another, our children and most especially our relationship with our God. Jesus told Martha: "you are so worried about so many things but only a few things are necessary". If husband and wife have so much going on in their lives that they are missing the happiness and joy of one another is it any wonder marriages end in divorce? More importantly if there is so much going on in your lives, you are missing the opportunity to enjoy the presence of God in your life. Many are like that even when they come to church. God's presence is all over the place and they can't benefit by it because they are so consumed with their schedules and what they "need to do" that they miss God!

Husbands and wives I really don't care what is currently going on in your life. I am telling you that your marriage is a treasure waiting to be discovered if you haven't already. A loving, Godly marriage is God's design and when both understand this and follow God's plan it is an awesome ride! What happens many times however, is marriages let the things of the world destroy what God has given to us as a wonderful gift. Of course money is one of the things that causes great stress in marriages and relationships in general. We let dollars or lack of them dominate our lives and our thoughts leaving little room for the joy of loving each other. Zechariah 4 tells us: "...To despise not the days of small *beginnings*". What this says to me is that we may need to live within our means. Wives when you have a husband that is providing for you make sure you are functioning within the boundaries of his abilities to provide and not get caught up in the "what other people have" mentality and cause stress in your marriage and life by living beyond your means. If wives or husbands do this the pressures I talked about before come into play and the relationship between the husband and wife will suffer. It is not in God's plan to live beyond your ability to pay for the way you live. If you do no matter how much money comes through the door more will go out and the marriage will suffer.

I know this might sound a bit odd, but even if there is plenty of money coming in, there is never a justification for wasting it. In a later chapter I am going to talk more about finances and the importance of them in a Heavenly marriage, but suffice it to say God's word tells us that we are to be good stewards of what He provides and we are not to waste it. I have seen many in my years of service who gain great wealth only to squander it away on meaningless toys and activities and to end up with nothing because they had made money the center of their lives and relationships rather than having God at the center of their lives. Many times in the Bible we see men and women who seem to have it all fall because they lose direction for their lives and begin to concentrate on the things of the world rather than the things of God.

Loving one another and having a strong marriage is important for many reasons but biblically we need to understand that marriage was to be a model for the church and because of this it would be safe to say that the condition of your marriage is bigger than you! The reason I say this is a defective marriage affects the kingdom because when a family is weak the church is weak. To exemplify this one can look to Paul and his letters to the church at Ephesus. He had stayed and established a church there for three years. The church was experiencing great growth and prosperity. Even with this Paul wrote to them to explain that to continue to take the church to the next level they needed to take their families and relationships to the next level. Simplistically to continue to further God's kingdom here on earth... husbands love your wives and wives love your husbands.

So what are some practical applications I can leave you with to assist you in making your marriage a Heavenly one rather than continuing to go through Hell?

1. Respect one another and the roles God has laid out for each of you in His word.

2. Marriage requires a mutual submission. With this it is impossible to think you are submitted if you are not willing to be accountable.

3. When you are challenged by your spouse, a good mate is not out to hurt you, they are out to enhance you.

4. Few things discourage a man more than when his wife shows more respect for her friends, relatives and co-workers than she does for her husband.

5. Husbands love your wives like Christ loved the church, then you can tolerate pain and the object of your love will respond.

6. Tolerate trouble and resolve it that is what it takes to restore a relationship. Christ was beaten and stripped, but he dealt with the embarrassment because he knew that change was coming.

7. Love each other as Christ loved the church and then neither of you will have to compete for time, because each will know they are a priority.

8. Understand than intimacy does not begin at night. It starts in the morning and lasts all day. Making love to one another is more than just indulging in each other's bodies. Make yours an on-going romance.

A pastor was once counseling a man during a time of trauma in a marriage. The pastor asked the man what he felt was the problem. The answer was, "I just don't love her any more".

The pastor answered, "Then love her".

The man then said, "But I don't love her".

The pastor then answered, "Then love her more".

It is not easy, but it is possible to love each other so much that a marriage can overcome the times it goes through Hell and be a Heavenly marriage. It does, however take work on the part of both the husband and wife and a constant cultivation to be successful. You have to make the conscious decision to "love" your spouse. Discuss together that you want to live your life together with what is biblically correct.

APPLICATION AND EXERCISES

1. How do you show your spouse how much you love them?

2. When was the last time you did something positive for your spouse that was totally unexpected and what was it?

3. Make a conscious effort to show affection towards your wife/husband outside the bedroom. Later ask them how it made them feel.

4. Discuss a time when you observed your parent(s) displaying affection for one another. How did that make you feel?

5. Did you ever see your parents fight? How did that make you feel?

6. Why is it important for you to model love for each other in front of your children and non-Christians?

7. Identify a couple in your life that has been married for at least ten years and ask them how they show love for one another.

8. Ask your spouse what one thing you could do to make them feel more valued and/or take a burden from them. Now do it!

9. Sometime each day pray for your spouse.

10. When you think about your spouse, what makes you smile?

CHAPTER 5

ADULTERY!
A SHORT TIME ACTION THAT
CAUSES LONG LASTING
CONSEQUENCES

2 SAMUEL 11:2-5

ONE EVENING DAVID GOT UP FROM HIS BED AND WALKED AROUND
ON THE ROOF OF THE PALACE. FROM THE ROOF HE SAW A WOMAN
BATHING. THE WOMAN WAS VERY BEAUTIFUL, 3 AND DAVID SENT
SOMEONE TO FIND OUT ABOUT HER. THE MAN SAID, "ISN'T THIS
BATHSHEBA, THE DAUGHTER OF ELIAM AND THE WIFE OF URIAH THE
HITTITE?" 4 THEN DAVID SENT MESSENGERS TO GET HER. SHE CAME
TO HIM, AND HE SLEPT WITH HER. (SHE HAD PURIFIED HERSELF FROM
HER UNCLEANNESS.) THEN SHE WENT BACK HOME. 5 THE WOMAN
CONCEIVED AND SENT WORD TO DAVID, SAYING, "I AM PREGNANT."

With recent media attention focusing on celebrities and
their marriage failures and indiscretions, it would be remiss
of me to avoid a discussion about the dangers associated
with unauthorized, illicit, and immoral relationships. We
live in a very sensuous society. We are to be in the world

but not of the world (John 17:14). The world wants us to walk in grey areas, areas where the lines between right and wrong are blurred and a person justifies his or her actions based on how they feel. Operating in the grey area can lead to satisfying feelings and fleshly emotions but we must stay faithful to God in singleness and marriage because there is no pain free ticket for the admission into fornication and adultery.

Nothing can destroy a family faster than the act of adultery. The only difference between the public relationships that are being played out in the media and the ones that everyday people are having is that they are being played out publicly for everyone to see, read about, and to judge. If I could ask these celebrities one question, I would ask, "Was it worth it?" I feel sure that most of them would admit that the costs (loss of relationships, personal and public embarrassment, loss of respect, etc.) were not worth the momentary pleasure they experienced from their decision to be unfaithful to their spouse and family.

I am reminded of a public official who, for months, denied having a relationship with a young intern. When he was called upon to answer whether he had engaged in an improper relationship with the woman, he replied, "I have had no sexual relations with that woman." Interestingly enough, how he defined that relationship is a problem that many people experience when they have "friendships" with individuals outside of their marriage. Is sharing intimate conversations, inappropriate? Is doing everything except engaging in "the act," inappropriate? Is it inappropriate to simply share a long hug? What about a kiss? Are any of these acts considered adultery?

The Bible is clear as to the answer to the question above, so let's define several terms that are important and what God's word tell us about them. *Adultery* is defined as "willful sexual intercourse with someone other than your wife or husband." Jesus expanded the definition of adultery to also include a "cultivation of lust." *Lust* is defined as an intense, obsessive, overwhelming, or unrestrained desire or cravings for anything that is contrary to what God wants us to have. An *unauthorized relationship* can be defined as *any* relationship with a person that you do not have the ability to be open about with your family and/or friends about. If you feel a need to lock or hide your phone, erase text messages, or go to another room when having a conversation with a "friend," you may be involved in an inappropriate, dangerous, willful, unhealthy, and sinful soul tie. An *unhealthy soul tie* is having a relationship with another person that is perverted or ungodly, and that keeps you from being free to become all that God intends for you to become. *Temptation* is the desire to do something enticing that you know you shouldn't, but want to. *Soul ties* can be healthy as well as unhealthy. When a person talks constantly with a person about their hopes and dreams, problems, disappointments, frustrations, joys and sorrows, they are actually relating on a soul level. The soul is made up of the mind, will, and emotions. So, when you are constantly talking to another person other than your spouse about the issues of life, you are developing an unhealthy soul tie that may be difficult even over a course of time. If you have a strong desire to talk to a person other than your spouse about your life issues, concerns, and problems, you may be involved in an emotional affair that has an unhealthy soul tie. If you have to hide the true nature of your relationship from your family and friends, you may be engaged in an unauthorized relationship even if the relationship is not one of a physical nature. Affairs can be physical as well as emotional. In these emotional relationships, coworkers or friends, start out having innocent conversations that end up taking them down a path of destruction that they neither anticipated nor wanted.

The enemy wants your heart! He tries to tempt us in order to dismantle us from God's will. He goes after your heart because he knows that most people are controlled by their emotions, feelings, and their desire to satisfy their flesh. The devil knows that if he can control you emotionally, then he can control you physically. Decisions that are made during emotional times and times of crisis have the potential of causing irreparable damage to even the strongest marriages.

Song of Solomon 2:15 warns, *"Catch for us the foxes, the little foxes that ruin the vineyards, our vineyards that are in bloom."* A look, a joke, a touch, or an inappropriate conversation has the potential of starting something that may compromise the integrity of a marriage. We must guard ourselves and our hearts against anyone or anything that may compromise the marriage and the vows of love taken on the wedding day. The small foxes can spoil the vine of love. Since there is never any room for compromise in the Kingdom, you must ask yourself "Is any relationship outside of my marriage worth me losing my family, my dreams, and my goals over?" Your reputation, security, and dreams can be destroyed overnight because of one short term decision for carnal pleasure that you thought no one would ever find out about.

As you recall, David made a decision to summon Bathsheba without any thought to the inevitable. During his emotional decision, he paid no thought to Bathsheba, his own position of power, his past or current successes and blessings, or the consequences of his actions. His thoughtless decision to act on his feelings caused an unexpected and unwanted pregnancy, pain, grief, guilt, recrimination from a friend, and ultimately death to Bathsheba's unsuspecting and innocent husband who served David loyally in battle. With all we know about David, it is apparent that during this time, he acted with spiritual immaturity and selfishness. In Matthew 5:28, Jesus says that *"whoever looks at a woman to lust after her has committed adultery with her in his heart."* So, with that first look (the small fox), David has already committed adultery. Not unlike in David's time, we are living in a time where it seems that few people possess the ability to control their flesh. The Bible is clear when it says that *"if we walk in the spirit, we will not fulfill the lust of the flesh."* Being spiritually mature means having the ability to exhibit self control in every situation.

The devil wants to trick us into thinking that none of the repercussions that adulterers face will happen to you. The trick of the enemy is to make you think that you are smarter than to get caught - because after all, you are much too smart to have it "go down like that." Regardless of how smart a person thinks he/she is, secret sins may escape the eyes of your family and friends for a season, but God not only sees, but considers all of our acts. God has a Heavenly camera that is shining Light on our actions. It is well known that our sins will find us out. Numbers 32:23 says, *"But if you fail to do this, you will be sinning against the Lord; and you may be sure that your sin will find you out"*. It is foolish to think that because no one knows about the secret sin, that God will turn His head against those acts. When we choose to sin, invariably it can only lead to destruction if we do not repent.

We should avoid even the appearance of impropriety in dealing with members of the opposite sex. Have you ever found yourself doing any of the following?

1. Having work meetings off-site with a member of the opposite sex?

2. Getting personal advice or personal counseling from a member of the opposite sex?

3. Talking to a member of the opposite sex about your marriage, concerns, or problems?

4. Allowing work conversations to extend too long?

5. Looking forward to before work, lunch-time, or break-time conversations or finding reasons to stop by their office or desk to say hello?

6. Looking for reasons to contact the person after hours to discuss work related issues?

7. Always looking forward to sitting beside the same person in meetings?

8. Tolerating flirtations, seeking/enjoying praise from a coworker, telling, listening to, and enjoying inappropriate stories or jokes?

9. Receiving or sending inappropriate email or text messages?

10. Riding to meetings together-just the two of you?

11. Calling the other person, just to check up or check in, or to see how they are doing?

12. Without your spouse's knowledge, approval, or input, serving as a mentor, friend, or big brother/sister to the child of the single parent?

While these may be totally innocent acts, we must avoid putting ourselves in situations that compromise our integrity or that may lead anyone else to believe something about us that is not true to our nature as Christian women and men.

Sometimes we look at others and wonder why anyone would cheat on their spouse? This is especially true when we look at those we discussed earlier in this chapter who are in the public eye and seem to have everything anyone would want; great career, beautiful and/or handsome spouse, money and fame. An answer may be that many times when a person cheats on their spouse, in their mind they feel perfectly justified by saying that their spouse is not around enough, they don't "feel the same about them anymore," or they feel they are not spending enough time together. But it seems to me that if you can find the time to cheat, you should be able to find the time to spend with your spouse.

As we return our focus on David, he went from being a virtual unknown to being well known. He went from a humble job where nobody knew him to a great job where everyone knew him. The enemy has a way of targeting successful people because if he can get successful people to fail, then other people who look up to them will be affected by their failure. In Revelations 12:4, we see that where the Word says, *"and his tail swept away a third of the starts of heaven, and threw them to the earth"*.

The following terms may clarify better some issues that cause spouses to look for gratification outside their marriage.

1. <u>Selfishness/narcissism</u> – individuals want what they want without any regard for their spouse or ultimately, their family. When selfishness, arrogance, ego, and opportunity overcome a person, he or she is unlikely to want to think of anything else. Once that thought takes root and opportunity presents itself, without God's help, this individual may even convince themselves that they have a "right" to have this relationship and will proceed without further thought to the consequences. Deciding to have an affair is a selfish, personal choice. No one can force you have an affair regardless of what you believe they have done (or have not done). The decision to have an affair is made because human beings are rewarded with the ability to make free will decisions.

2. <u>Time and Opportunity</u> – Did you know that more pregnancies take place during the spring than any other time of the year? There are certain seasons when the enemy intensifies his attach against our lives. We must be careful to avoid sedentary lifestyles and being idle. Where we have too much time on our hands, the enemy has an opportunity to infiltrate our

minds with useless, distracting, and inappropriate thoughts. The enemy will set you up if you are not careful to avoid placing yourself in compromising situations. For example, why was Bathsheba taking a bath on the roof? I have found during my study time that in Palestine, the roof was used as a sitting or resting place. Is it possible that Bathsheba had an agenda when she went to the roof to bathe? If she avoided taking a bath on the roof in the first place, she would not have been seen by David. However, if David refused to watch a woman taking a bath on the roof when he should have been in battle with his army, then he would not have compromised himself. David failed to see how this one act of disobedience was going to destroy and negatively impact every area of his life. We note in 1st and 2nd Samuel that David's short term decision to sleep with Bathsheba caused one disaster after another; including rape, murder, and revolt (those long lasting consequences)!!!

3. Lack of appreciation for what they have at home. The old adage, "The grass is greener on the other side of the fence," is so misleading that it often causes men and women to seek outside relationships because of this perception. However, as Bishop T D Jakes says, "grass is greener where you water it." An overall lack of appreciation for what is at home will open the door for adulterous relationships. The Bible says that it is important for a man to remember the wife of his youth so that he may enjoy continual blessings (Proverbs 5:18).

4. <u>Boredom</u>. An often cited complaint about marriage is that spouses say that the marriage or their spouse has become boring or unexciting. When a person becomes bored, they lose their mental edge. As a result, their mind will lead them into places where they should not wander. We must take our bored and sinful thoughts captive (2 Corinthians 10:4-5) and stop the sin before it festers in our hearts and in our minds. One way to avoid boredom in the marriage is to continue seeing the good in your spouse. You should also begin dating your spouse again. Find ways to reenergize and rebuild the marriage in ways that work for both spouses. Dating your spouse has to become a priority because life's issues and pressures have a way of overwhelming a couple if they are not intentional and committed to keeping the marriage alive and exciting.

5. <u>The Thrill of Secrecy</u> is an attraction for some because many times the secrecy is a part of the overall fantasy and reward for sneaking around and not getting caught. For some, sneaking around to create opportunities for these "flings" is as fun and erotic as having the affair itself. This type of thinking can only lead to destruction.

6. <u>Affirmation of their Self Image</u> – Men may seek the "chase" and "challenge" of an affair to affirm that they "still have it." A man may have a need to validate his successes in life beyond his job. In some cases if a man does not feel successful in his professional life,

he may seek success in other areas, including "the chase" with women that may affirm his self image. Women, on the other hand, have a need to feel loved, appreciated, and valued. If she feels inadequate in any way, she may look outside the marriage to affirm her perceived self image as well. Women may be enticed to have an extramarital affair because a man tells her repeatedly those things that her husband may not be telling her at home. Her male coworker may make her feel admired and beautiful, thus using these words as tricks of the devil to encourage her to sin against the marriage vows.

7. Mid-life Crises – sometimes when men and women reach middle age (40-60's), they look back over their lives and wish they had done more. They may fear growing older and too often they feel like they have missed out of some important aspects of their life. They may feel like failures in certain areas and attempt to recreate or "spice-up" their lives by having affairs, or engaging in other dangerous or age inappropriate acts.

8. Hanging Out with Unmarried Friends or Married Friends who Cheat – The likelihood of a man (or woman) being unfaithful to their spouse is heightened when an individual has lots of unmarried friends or friends to glamorize cheating on their spouses. Hanging around spouses who cheat makes cheating seem like the "norm." So, it is important to befriend as many happily married couple- friends as possible.

Regardless of the reason for engaging in relationships outside of your marriage, it is sin and will not go unpunished. The Bible has much to say about adultery and the consequences for those who commit adultery. Always remember that adultery may start sweet but will always end in bitterness.

May I take the time to share some specific scriptures that speak to what we have discussed?

- You shall not commit adultery. (Exodus 20:14)

- Why be captivated, my son, by an adulteress? Why embrace the bosom of another man's wife? (Proverbs 5:20)

- He who commits adultery with a woman is void of understanding. He who does it destroys his own soul. (Proverbs 6:32)

- You have heard that it was said, 'You shall not commit adultery; 28 but I tell you that everyone who gazes at a woman to lust after her has committed adultery with her already in his heart. (Matthew 5:27-28)

- Let marriage be held in honor among all, and let the bed be undefiled: but God will judge the sexually immoral and adulterers. (Hebrews 13:4)

- With eyes full of adultery, they never stop sinning; they seduce the unstable; they are experts in greed— an accursed brood! (2 Peter 2:14)

- So I will cast her on a bed of suffering, and I will make those who commit adultery with her suffer intensely, unless they repent of her ways. (Revelation 2:22)

So now you are reading this and saying that I just don't understand and that you are different and all the scriptures and ramifications are right on for everyone else, but not necessarily you, correct? Well, that is just not true! The sin of adultery is much like being dead. What I mean by that is that if you're dead you're dead. You can't be any more or less dead. It is the same with adultery. If you have committed adultery, then there are no levels of it. You will pay the consequences. Some more thoughts;

1. You can choose your sinful act but you cannot choose the consequences of those choices. Our own sinful choices impacts generations after us to the 3rd and 4th generation.

2. When couples stay together after adultery, adultery can be forgiven but is never forgotten; adultery scars reputations, creates distrust, ill will, bitterness and resentment.

3. Adultery may lead to Divorce:
   a. Breaks up marriages and families
   b. Shatters dreams and breaks hearts

4. Deprives children of a sense of financial and emotional security and well being.
   a. Sale of the family home
   b. Expenses involved in maintaining two separate households for mother and father

5. Causes children to think that the breakup was somehow their fault

6. Children lack full time access to non-custodial parent

7. Relationships of non-custodial parents and children often suffer

8. Often leaves women and children in lower states of financial stability than husbands

9. Creates a sense of distrust for children in their future relationships

10. Loss of couple/family relationships and friendships-affects neighbors and whose choices become avoidance, defense, or rationalization.

11. Marriages consummated in adultery are rarely successful.

A logical question should be how can I be assured my marriage will not end up in divorce because of an adulterous relationship? While there are no guarantees because we can only control ourselves and not others, there are some practical things we can do and I will discuss those in the next chapter. I will also discuss in an upcoming chapter what to do if you have already fallen into this Hell trap of adultery and how you can possibly bring your marriage back to a Heavenly one.

APPLICATION/DISCUSSION

1. With David being described as "A man after God's own heart", how could he allow himself to be involved in the trap of adultery? Do you know any David like people in your own sphere of influence?

2. What does the Bible tell us we are to do if we find ourselves in a situation like the ones described in this chapter where a coworker begins to discuss very personal issues with us, puts us in situations where we feel uncomfortable or tell us off color jokes or stories?

3. Discuss a recent personality who has been caught cheating and what have the ramifications of that adulterous act had on him/her?

4. Has an adulterous affair affected your own family or extended family? What was the effect on the people themselves, the children and others?

5. After having read this chapter, what one thing will you do differently than you have done before?

CHAPTER 6

FORGIVENESS: THE ART OF LEARNING TO LET GO

PHILIPPIANS 3:13

BROTHERS, I DO NOT CONSIDER MYSELF YET TO HAVE TAKEN HOLD OF
IT. BUT ONE THING I DO: FORGETTING WHAT IS BEHIND AND STRAINING
TOWARD WHAT IS AHEAD."

One of the greatest challenges that couples face is in the area of forgiveness. I believe that learning how to forgive your spouse early in your marriage will set the stage for how happy, whole, and healthy your marriage becomes as the years progress. The earlier couples learn to forgive, the easier that correction and reconciliation become the norm in the relationship throughout the marriage.

God is so serious about forgiveness in the life of Christians that He provides a mandate (required in order to receive forgiveness) and a model (Christ is our model) so that we would know why forgiveness is important and how we are to forgive. Couples find it difficult to forgive one another because they are often guilty of keeping records and mental lists of sins, hurts, words, and even sinful or hurtful intentions against each other. We are all required to forgive, especially when we do not "feel" like it. Many times, couples find it difficult to forgive because they had one offense, one hurt, and one unkind word on top of the next offense until the list of offenses becomes so large that the marriage crumbles under its weight. First Corinthians 13 says, *"Love keeps no record of wrong."* You and I have been called to reflect the image of God in everything we do and that includes forgiving people that have hurt us. You might be thinking, "But Pastor Ramsey, you don't know what they did to me." That's true, I don't know what they did to you, but I do know what not forgiving can do to you. I know it isn't a word but I call this "unforgiveness". This unforgiveness holds you hostage to the memory of the hurt or offense. Many times when we have been hurt, we fail to see that unforgiveness often does more damage than the offense that hurt you in the first place. I say that because unforgiveness holds you hostage to what that person did to you. More than that, it is possible to be out of a situation but still bound by the memory of it. The reality of unforgiveness is that it empowers those people who may no longer be in your life. If you choose not to forgive that person, you are actually giving that person permission and a license to control your thoughts, your actions, and even your emotions. If you find yourself upset at the thought or mention of that person's name, trust me, you have not forgiven them. Don't misunderstand; I won't minimize how you feel or the effects of those actions on you personally and emotionally. Yes, I know that some people have a way of hurting you so bad that you think you won't ever recover. But it's during those trying times, that you have to lean on God even more.

God commands us to forgive so that He can forgive our sins. *"And when you stand praying, if you hold anything against anyone, forgive him, so that your Father in heaven may forgive you your sins" (Mark 11:25)*. You see, God obviously knew that we wouldn't forgive easily. He had to remind us that we all have sinned and fallen short of His glory (Romans 3:23). So, if we expect and desire God to forgive us, how can we withhold forgiveness from a brother or sister that needs our forgiveness, our fellowship, and/or our travel fare? Would we withhold from them, the very thing that God has freely given us?

Another condition that God places on forgiveness is related to how many times we should forgive a person that sins against us. In Matthew 18:21-22 Peter came to the Lord and asked the question, *"Lord, how often shall my brother sin against me, and I forgive him?"* We have all asked this question at some point in our lives. We have to fully consider our motives in the asking of the question. What do we really want to know? Do we really want to know the answer or are we trying to justify not forgiving the person. Jesus said to Peter, *"I do not say to you, up to seven times, but up to seventy times seven."*

I wonder if Peter really wanted to know a number of times he should forgive or if he was trying to ask, "How long do I have to take this?" You see, when Peter first came to Jesus in modern day vernacular what Peter was really saying was "How long do I have to put up with this craziness"? His motivation for asking the question was not forgiveness, it was likely revenge. It is my opinion that Peter wanted to know how long he had to "take this" before a fleshly response to the pain happened. So, in essence, Jesus responded to Peter's question by saying, "No, not seven times but seventy times seven". This response was not what Peter was looking for because it forced him to rethink, how long you choose to hang on to an offense. The point is that anyone that would go through the trouble of keeping track of 490 offenses and then feel justified to hurt the offender has a bigger problem than the one that caused your pain. So many people decide not to forgive because they believe the person that hurt them will get away with it. We must allow God to take care of our feelings of hurt, betrayal, and revenge (Psalm 147:3) and also to take care of the person that hurt us if He chooses (Romans 12:19-21).

I have counseled couples who have recounted offenses made by their spouse so long and with such passion that it made me wonder if the offense happened that week. When I asked the person when that particular event happened, I found that the hurt or sin had happened years before, but the person was holding on to it so tight and could recite and recount every detail. This is clearly a case of unresolved anger turned into bitterness and unforgiveness that needs to be dealt with. Without forgiveness, the bitterness will ultimately destroy your relationships and ability to serve God effectively (Hebrews 12:15). It will put your marriage in Hell or be the cause of the marriage actually ending.

In another context, Jesus teaches in a sermon on

forgiveness that is birthed out of the actions of an angry believer. We all know that Peter had no problem fighting, cursing or cutting someone when he was questioned, felt attacked, or even when he felt the need to defend Jesus. This was proven in the garden and the three times that Peter denied knowing Jesus (Matthew 26:69-75). Like He did with Peter, Jesus has to help us deal with our issues. He has to bring us to a place where we recognize and acknowledge our true selves, where we can see the ugliness, anger, and bitterness in our hearts. Jesus had to help Peter deal with his anger issues and emotional responses to things that happened to him in life. If Jesus hadn't helped Peter, he would never have been able to reach his full potential. Where does that leave you with unresolved issues? Are there things or people that you need to deal with before you can reach your destiny? Although Peter felt extremely embarrassed about denying Jesus, he regained his momentum and ultimately went on to do greater works. He did not sit around crying about denying Jesus, beating himself up for his actions, or feeling sorry for himself. He ultimately knew he had been forgiven and took the restoration of himself to Jesus to heart.

In the case of the Prodigal Son (Luke 15:11-32), more often than not, we hear the story of the son who left his father's house after demanding his inheritance. But, I want to focus on the brother that stayed home. Although this brother stayed home, worked hard for his father, and served well, was unforgiving and resentful of his younger brother. In my words, the older brother all but screamed, "What about me? I did all this work and now you throw him a party. Ain't that a trip?" In spite of everything he did that was good, his anger, resentment, and bitterness overshadowed the welcomed relief his father felt having his younger son home.

Unfortunately, the older brother became a willing victim. The older brother assumed that his father's gift of reconciliation for the younger brother was a slight to him personally. No doubt he felt insulted, slighted, and rejected by the father whom he served without interruption. However, he assumed a "holier than my brother" attitude about his father when approached about his absence at the party celebrating the younger brother's return.

Forgiveness requires the submission of your feelings, emotions, and thoughts. In many cases, forgiveness means that you are required to confess your honest desire to hold on to the anger, resentment, and hostility toward a particular person. You have to ask yourself, "Why am I holding on to the hurt? What benefit am I getting from still being mad about this issue? Most often it will take Divine help and intervention to move you to a place where you know you that the only way you can forgive that person is with God's help.

Proverbs 18:19 describes a person who is so offended that they will not forgive. The scripture says that "An offended brother is more unyielding than a fortified city, and disputes are like the barred gates of a citadel." Notice that the text compares being offended to an unyielding fortified city. Unforgiveness causes people to be unyielding, inflexible and unwilling to change. The only way to get into that fortified city is to come up with a military strategy to get past the walls. Unforgiveness causes you to put up walls and be suspicious of everyone that comes into your life. And if you are not careful, you will find yourself rejecting the very people that God is trying to send into your life whether it is a potential mate, friend, or a counselor.

It is important to understand what forgiveness is and what it is not. Forgiveness does not mean the immediate and complete restoration of trust. If someone comes to my house for a visit, steals something from us while they are there, but before they get home, the Lord convicts them of their wrong and they return to my house, confess their sin, repent, and return the item. Now what do you think I ought to do? If you said that I would immediately forgive them, you would be right. Don't get it twisted though. I would immediately forgive them for stealing from us and for compromising our trust. But, it is highly likely that they will not be invited back to our house for a long time, if ever. Does that mean that I have not forgiven them? No, I have forgiven them, but forgiveness does not mean the restoration of trust at the moment that the person asks for forgiveness. Trust takes seconds to lose, but often takes a long time to rebuild. That person would have to regain and re-earn my trust if they ever had a chance of the relationship being what it used to be. As Bishop Hilliard says, "Repentance will put you back in the line, but not necessarily at the front of the line". Sometimes the relationship may never be restored to the place it was at the beginning. You have to know that sometimes relationships need to be redefined in order to be better.

If you are going to have that marriage made in Heaven, you cannot allow these problems to rob you of the faith you need to change it and forgive your spouse. You must have God at the center of your marriage and have a vision of what you want your marriage to be. Proverbs 29:18 says, "Where there is no vision, the people perish: but he that keeps the law, happy is he." A successful marriage is one that has the vision to take the marriage where God would want it to go, not where the individuals or the world would want.

Vision is defined as the act or power of anticipating that which will or may come to pass. It is the ability to vividly see an event in your mind that has yet to happen in reality. Too often those who have been hurt are looking in the rear view mirror rather than having a vision of how to forgive and make their marriage what it should and they want it to be. Having this vision is critical to a successful marriage as well as a successful life in general. Without this vision marriage is like a swamp with no boundaries and no direction, but with a clear vision, a Heavenly marriage is like a beautiful river with direction, productive and filled with life. Too many couples believe that marriage is to be tolerated (swamp) instead of being celebrated (river). God's plan all the way back to Adam and Eve shows us that marriage was meant to bless your life and not stress your life. Keeping track of old issues and keeping the baggage of unforgiveness weights down the marriage rather than uplifting it.

What I am saying here is that every relationship, including your relationship with God, has to continue to be cultivated in order to reach its potential. A farmer can't simply plant a crop and go back in the fall and harvest a successful bounty. He has to continue to cultivate, get rid of the weeds and pray to God for the blessings. It is exactly the same with a marriage. We have to get rid of the weeds and continue to nurture the relationship to make sure the marriage grows into a Heavenly one. What I see for many believers is the moment they experience a difficulty in the marriage (a weed), they allow the enemy to convince them that the situation will never change. The moment they buy into that lie, they become what I call "marital martyrs". In other words they take on the mentality that they are just going to suffer through the marriage for the kingdom's sake. What they fail to realize is that if they would use the same faith that they are using to endure, they could come out of the situation by letting God change them and their circumstances.

The logical question should be, "Pastor, why do things like unforgiveness, adultery, and fornication happen in a marriage, especially one with Christians being equally yoked?" The answer of course goes all the way back to the beginning scripture about David. The enemy will always try to attack any family that is reaching its potential in God because you have become a model of God's relationship to the church. Please don't misunderstand, I am not saying that because you have a Heavenly marriage and are doing God's will that it is a guarantee that one of the spouses is going to do something drastically wrong to harm the marriage. What I am saying is that the enemy will try and attack if given an opening to do so. The family needs to put on the full amour of God (Ephesians 6) to be ready to fight off the evil one. The enemy doesn't have to waste the time destroying marriages and relationships of the un-Godly. He already has them. I am convinced he goes after the saved so he can use his evil ways to trap more unsuspecting victims. Just always be on guard against the evil one and be sure that your marriage and family are on the solid rock of God's word. To put into my words, "you need to have the tools to storm proof your house".

To finish up this chapter on forgiveness I would like to leave you with ten statements that if taken to heart and lived on a daily basis could positively affect your Heavenly marriage. This Heavenly marriage gives you an opportunity to see how legitimate your Christianity really is. I say that because everything it takes to be a good Christian are the same ingredients that it takes to have a great marriage.

1. Honesty and openness-"Adam and Eve were naked"

2. Willingness to admit wrong and repent

3. Consistent communication-"men ought always to be in prayer"

4. A willingness to change-"you have to be willing to dethrone your flesh"

5. A willingness to be corrected

6. A non-negotiable commitment

7. Consistently praise

8. If you quit moving for the better is at the risk of your personal happiness

9. Press to maturity

10. Your commitment to getting in the presence of God is what will give you the ability to tolerate the presence of others.

Too often we want to put all the blame on others and never look at ourselves. We always look to others and wait for them to change. If the marriage is in Hell because of any issue, perhaps you being the first to make a move to God and trust him for restoration would be the first move in navigating to the Heavenly marriage you have as a vision. To put this in perspective let me share a personal experience.

Recently we were in Houston. I admit that when I am out of my comfort zone and in an area that I am not familiar with, I become directionally challenged. Therefore, each time I rent a car, I rent one that has a navigation system in it. Where we were, I had driven from the hotel to the church many times, but I still used the navigation system to get me to my destination because I had not remembered the names of the roads. One night on the way to the church service the navigation system stopped working. So my wife and I struggled to get to our destination. We finally made it, but not without a great deal of stress and uncertainty. I was angry and stressed, but when I finally calmed down and thought about it was evident it was not the navigation system's problem alone. My trouble was caused because I was depending on someone (something) else to get me there instead of taking the responsibility myself. It is exactly the same with forgiveness. We must make the move to navigate through the swamps of life and live as God directs us if we reach our vision for a marriage of Heavenly proportions.

DISCUSSION/APPLICATION

1. Discuss a situation/incident where you have seen evidence of unforgiveness affecting a family and/or marriage.

2. Discuss a situation/incident where you have seen evidence of forgiveness in a marriage and the outcome of the forgiveness.

3. Have you ever been hurt by someone who was supposed to be your friend? How did you personally handle the situation?

4. Whose responsibility is it to forgive and why?

5. You must also be able to forgive yourself as well as others who have wronged you. Take the time to write on a piece of paper at least five times you have been hurt or have hurt others. Now take the paper, wad it up and shred or burn it.

CHAPTER 7

HEAVEN IN YOUR HOUSE

JOSHUA 24:15

BUT IF SERVING THE LORD SEEMS UNDESIRABLE TO YOU, THEN
CHOOSE FOR YOURSELVES THIS DAY WHOM YOU WILL SERVE, WHETHER
THE GODS YOUR FOREFATHERS SERVED BEYOND THE RIVER, OR THE
GODS OF THE AMORITES, IN WHOSE LAND YOU ARE LIVING. BUT AS
FOR ME AND MY HOUSEHOLD, WE WILL SERVE THE LORD.

All of us at one time or another have wondered why we do certain things or act a certain way. I want to attempt to explain why certain types of behavior patterns exist within many of our families. The Bible declares that the sins of the fathers are visited upon the sons to the third and fourth generations. I suggest to you that there will come a time in your life where you have to fight your daddy's devil! If you do not realize this and fight those devils, your marriage will most likely not be a heavenly one. Examine yourself and your family.

- If you can look at your family and see several generations of pregnancy outside of wedlock; I want to suggest to you that is not just an act, that's a spirit.

- If you can look at your family and see several generations of addiction; that is not just an act, that's spirit.

- If you can look at your family and see several generations of welfare; I want to suggest to you that it is not just a difficult time, it is a spirit.

- If you can look at your family and see a lack of education; I want to suggest to you that is also a spirit. I once knew a family that had five kids and not one of them graduated from high school. You must know that ignorance will limit your personal potential!

- If you can look at your family and see several generations of lazy and irresponsible men; I suggest to you that is spirit because if the head is out of place, the rest of the family is dysfunctional!

What I have found is that many families continue in these downward cycles because they don't come to grips with the fact there are problems in their home. They believe it is "normal" and therefore they don't change and have happiness, joy and abundance in their lives. You see when it comes to sin, I have discovered that as long as you like what you do, you will never change what you do. Many people and families go through cycles of sin because they don't really want to give it up. Here is my little saying about the sin in some families and homes;

They do it.

They regret it.

They repent of it

The guilt leaves.

They repeat it!

How do you fight this tendency to repeat the sins of those before you? Well one of my favorite statements is, "When it comes to deliverance, you have to remember that persistence will distort resistance"! Being purposeful and persistent will allow you to overcome these habits from your past and allow your home to be different.

Why is it so important to have your home be a Godly one and your marriage to be a Heavenly one. Well, God's word makes the importance of this abundantly clear in Matthew 12:29. It says, *"Or again, how can anyone enter a strong man's house and carry off his possessions unless he first ties up the strong man? Then he can rob his house".* The implication of this text is this, when you and your house are bound up in sin, the enemy can do what he wants to in your house and your marriage. You must constantly (persistently) be clothed in God's word and have the Holy Spirit guiding your life and your home.

The logical question is how can I do better than I have before and what are some specific things I can do? Well, what I have found in my years in ministry I will tell you that what you don't appreciate will depreciate. What I mean by this is again you must constantly work on your Heavenly marriage and spend time in affirmation, thanksgiving and prayer.

What I have seen over the last 20 years is the devil intensifies his attack against the institution of marriage and family. One of the ways he begins to erode the fabric of the family is by causing spouses to fail to appreciate what God has given them. I speak not of material things but of the gift of each other and their children. Let me give you a personal illustration. A friend of mine gave me an expensive watch. It was given to me on a special day. Therefore it is not just that it has value in a material sense, but I value it because of when it was given, how it was given and the person who gave it to me. Because of all these things and especially my love for the person who gave me the gift I take care of it. It is a joy to have and not just because of its monetary value. I tell you this story because this precious gift given to me can symbolize the precious gift God has given you, your spouse.

It says in God's word in Proverbs 18 that "he that finds a wife finds a good thing, and obtains favor from the Lord". If God has given you a spouse, He has given you a gift of much more value than the watch given to me, but just like the watch you have a responsibility to value, protect and appreciate the gift God has given you. If you don't the chances are your relationship will depreciate just like the watch would if not taken care of in an appropriate manner.

It seems to me that one of the problems is that many of us just don't understand how and what to do to appreciate our home and families. What we don't seem to understand is;

- just because you are married doesn't mean you know how to be married

- just because you have had sex doesn't mean you know how to make love

- just because you have children doesn't mean you know how to be a parent
- just because you make money doesn't mean you know how to handle it.

What I have seen is that to a great degree we have become Christians in a cardiac culture and we have gotten so caught up in trying to provide for the house that we have failed to spend time with the people in the house. What we have to realize is that real love is the desire to give benefit to others even at the expense of one's self. What I see many times in marriages and relationships that end up in Hell is that lust takes over as the desire to benefit one's self at the expense of others. That will bankrupt the marriage and family quickly.

God does give us direction and mandates as far as our homes are concerned. In the Lord's prayer He says, ... "on earth as it is in Heaven". Based on this statement we understand that it is the will of God for us to experience "Heaven on earth". Since this is true that means that God expects there to be some Heaven in our houses. He also give us all the scriptures we need and the direction we need to be sure this is possible in our marriages and family. The enemy also knows all of this and will try and tear down a marriage and home if at all possible. One of the things I like to show people is from Ephesians 16. In verses 25-33 God compares His love of the church to the love of a wife. Let me break this down for you as an example of how spouses should love one another.

1. Christ said of the church... "I will never leave you nor forsake you"

2. He gave of Himself and gave his life even when we had nothing to offer Him

3. The scriptures tell us that God is always in His house... this tells us the importance of the presence of both spouses in the home

4. He tells us the church is not perfect but He will work to remove the spots and blemishes just the way we should work on our marriages.

So to end up this chapter let me tell you what I believe each of the two spouses need to be able to have a successful marriage, a Heavenly one. Four things that the woman has got to have;

1. Communication

2. Honesty

3. Financial support

4. Family commitment

We have touched on each of these, but I believe them to be paramount in a Heavenly marriage. The man is a bit more simple.

1. Sex (sorry ladies, but it is the truth)

2. Praise... I know this may seem selfish, but read the comparison God gives and you will understand.

I want to end this chapter with one more thought. No matter what you and/or your marriage has been through, you can make into a Heavenly one. All you need to do is to look to Noah for an example. If a man can build an arc when it isn't raining and take all the criticism from family and friends, then weather the greatest storm in history only to come out of it with his marriage and family intact, then how can we say it is not possible for our marriage and family to be successful?

DISCUSSION/APPLICATION

1. What is the difference between a house and a home?

2. Do you know a family who you believe to have a Heavenly home and family that could be an example? What makes them so special?

3. How can a spouse be lovingly held accountable for the Biblical roles in the family?

4. Characterize your family to an inanimate object. An example might be the family is a housing addition. All houses are of different ages and sizes, but all have the same foundations, the belief in Christ as their savior.

5. Husbands, knowing what your wife needs, how will you treat her differently?

6. Wives, knowing what you husband needs and what God directs, how will you treat him differently?

CHAPTER 8

CHILDREN: BLESSING OR BURDEN?

MATTHEW 19:14-15

JESUS SAID, "LET THE LITTLE CHILDREN COME TO ME, AND DO
NOT HINDER THEM, FOR THE KINGDOM OF HEAVEN BELONGS TO
SUCH AS THESE." WHEN HE HAD PLACED HIS HANDS ON THEM,
HE WENT ON FROM THERE.

In my years in the ministry I have seen and heard many
reasons for people to feel their marriage is in trouble and
rather than being heavenly they believe they are going
through hell. All the reasons for the tragedy of divorce are
disturbing, but the most disturbing to me is when children
are involved and sometimes blamed for the problems in the
marriage. Before I go any farther I want all who read this
book to understand this, "children belong to God and we
only are their caretakers". The sooner we comprehend this
fact and internalize our charge of taking care of God's gift
the better off we will be.

It never ceases to amaze me how some people don't

understand the blessing of children and look at raising children as a burden. Just the other night on our local news there were at least three news stories where children were abandoned, lost, stolen, abused or even killed by those who had been entrusted with caring for them. I know that we are not supposed to feel wrath towards others and that God will take care of punishment for sin not confessed, but when I hear and see grown men and women mistreat children it goes to the core of my soul. How any human being can treat a child in that manner is beyond my human comprehension. When and if a couple comes to me and begin to tell me how their children are causing the problems in their marriage I have to bring them quickly back to the word of God and lead them back to the fact that God loans us His children and we are to be the caretakers of them.

A good scripture for all of us to remember comes from Matthew 18:5-6. Christ makes it very clear what our charge as parents is and the ramifications of not meeting this charge.

> *And whoever welcomes a little child like this in my name welcomes me. But if anyone causes one of these little ones who believe in me to sin, it would be better for him to have a large millstone hung around his neck and to be drowned in the depths of the sea.*

I think all who believe their children to be a burden in their marriage should dwell on Christ's word and think long and hard about the ramifications of not caring for the gift(s) they were given by their heavenly father.

Please don't misunderstand. I know that raising children

is tough and many times you may sit and dream of how the empty nest will be once the kids are out of the house and on their own. That is normal and the tough times are not fun to go through, but it is our duty and responsibility to raise the children in a loving, caring home and not let them believe they are a millstone around our neck, lest we end up with one around ours.

I can just imagine some who are reading these words saying, "it is evident he just doesn't understand and he hasn't had to raise our kids". No, I haven't had to raise yours, and don't want to, but we are raising ours and I can speak with some authority as to the challenges of raising three very unique and distinct children. I will speak more about them a bit later.

Another issue I see in families is when a couple has a blended family. What I mean by this term is when a husband and wife marry and there are children from a former relationship. It does not matter what the issues were in the original marriage; divorce, death of a spouse, or a child out of wedlock. The issue of blending families seems to be very difficult in many cases and sometimes a marriage can quickly go to the Hell side because of these issues if they are not prayerfully addressed and tackled in a very real and direct manner. No matter how those children came into the family and no matter what the family structure looks like, they are still God's children and we still have the command to provide for them and lovingly raise them to adulthood.

Anyone in a situation where there are children in the home who are not biologically theirs may at times be frustrated and feel the children are not their responsibility.

That is not the case. Once the marriage takes place those children are your responsibility under God's word and you are to love them as your own and cherish them. You are to direct them and guide them. A perfect example of what you are to do is Joseph, Jesus' earthly father. Can you imagine if your wife came to you and told you the story that Mary told Joseph? What did he do? He trusted God and he trusted Mary and he raised and loved Jesus as his own. What a powerful example for us to follow!

But pastor, you don't understand how frustrated I get with these kids and how frustrated they get with me. It just seems to spiral out of control until we all get exasperated! If in a blended family, do you sometimes just say to yourself, "these aren't my kids so why do I have to worry about them?" Remember what I said in the very first paragraph of this chapter, no children are ours, they belong to God and we are only the caretakers. So, no matter whether they are your biological children or not, you are still to love them and not get frustrated or frustrate them. God's word in Matthew once again in Chapter 6:4 gives us a command,

> *"Fathers, do not exasperate your children; instead, bring them up in the training and instruction of the Lord."*

You might be able to sense that I am passionate about children being a blessing and not a burden. Perhaps you can understand why when I tell you about my own family. I am blessed in many ways, but one of my largest blessings from God is the children He is allowing my wife and me to nurture into adults. We are not what most would call a normal nuclear family. God has blessed us and we have chosen to celebrate diversity in our family.

My wife and children are the center of my world. The ministry revolves around them; I do not make them revolve around the ministry. I tell preachers all the time you don't want your children to grow up resenting your calling to full-time ministry. I believe the resentment happens because children grow up seeing their daddy go and meet the needs of the congregation but yet he cannot attend their games and/or school events. Why should they want to serve a God that took their parent(s) away from them? It is hard to explain to a ten year old why their father and/or mother have time for everyone and everything but them.

Alicia and I never really discussed the number of children we wanted to have before we got married. My wife is the oldest siblings of four with no sisters and I am the youngest of five with both sisters and brothers. I knew I didn't want five children and she didn't want four, so I think it was an unspoken that "two" was our magic number. After one year of marriage we were ready to start our family. I imagined we would have two healthy children preferably a boy and a girl. My son would love sports like me and my daughter would be a "girly girl" like her mother. I saw myself working hard and giving my family the things that I never had growing up. I knew just like my older brothers, that I would be a "hands on" father with both of my children. Now, here we are 15 ½ years later and I am blessed to have three beautiful, vivacious, and uniquely different children. Each one has brought something different into our home because they each entered into our world so differently.

Our first son, John Jr. aka Johnny was born healthy, handsome, and full of personality. Our second child a son, Jeremiah David, aka Jay was diagnosed inutero with a series of serious health challenges. Jeremiah's journey is a book of its own, yet I can't wait to share the joy that this handsome, artistic young man has brought into our lives. Our third child "the chosen one" a daughter, Judah Maree, aka Juice was adopted at birth and has already taken over my heart which those big beautiful dark brown eyes. Are my children a blessing or a burden?

I remember the day like it was yesterday when my wife went into labor with our first child. I began smiling on the inside as soon as we left the first ultra sound that confirmed it was a boy. The feeling of seeing your wife give birth to your first child is a feeling that cannot be described in just one or even two words. My son, whom we named John Fitzgerald Ramsey Jr., was born on October 11, 1997. My wife who is not in the least way over spiritual told me that God confirmed the name when she wasn't sure about it. The Lord told her that if she named him after me he would "double" all of the accomplishments that I achieved in life. Now let's fast forward to 2011 and we are already beginning to see the manifestation in John Jr. whom I also refer to as #1 son. He looks "just" like me, he wears glasses like me, he has to fight for his academic success like me, and his athletic ability at the age of 13 is prodigious sometimes indescribable which is better than me.

I began playing football when I was six years old. I knew at an early age that I would excel at football and track because I loved the game of football and I enjoyed running. The discipline that I showed at an early age for working out and studying the game was uncommon. As a senior at Snyder High School in Ft. Wayne, I had the privilege of being recruited by several top athletic programs. I accepted a full ride to Miami of Ohio on a football and track scholarship. I share this background with you because we are already starting to see the manifestation in our oldest child. John Jr. started playing football at age six. At the age of six he also began taking Tae Kwando. He started winning local sparing matches in local competitions and by the age of ten he received his black belt. Johnny won the National Tae Kwando championship in his age bracket at the age of ten, the first for the KTA studio lead by Master Cottie. He also received MVP for his football travel team due to his scoring ability and great sportsmanship.

He and I were both excited when track season started in the 6th grade. This would be his first time running track and I couldn't wait to see the similarities' he and I shared in our running style. At the first meet I could see in his stride the confidence he held while running against 8th graders. It was amazing how I could see myself in his facial expressions and mannerisms before he participated in his event. By the time he entered into the 7th grade to play football for his school team, he was prepared and dominated in various positions. He has already caught the attention of the high school and he wants to excel in all positions, something I never had the opportunity to do. He has already in my eyes accomplished double in his middle school years.

Seeing his athletic ability at such a young age caused me great joy but also caused a change in my work schedule because I wanted to help shape his athleticism. That meant that I needed to take him to his practices, attend his competitions, and stay in communication with his coaches.

Parenting was designed to be a partnership. My wife and I agree that when one redirects a child and/or gives consequences that the other parent must support it. Johnny found out very early in life that he could not run to one parent and try to undo what the other parent set in place. Whenever he comes to me with a request, I automatically ask "what did your mother say?"... If he hasn't asked her the same question he knows I will not make a decision until she and I have agreed on it. So now that he is a pre-teen he already knows the "flow" of our family and how decisions are made regarding his best interest. The bible states clearly in Proverbs 22:6, to train up a child in the way that he should go and when he is old he will not depart from it.

When our oldest son was two, we decided we wanted to have another child. My wife had just started her Master's in Education program so we just decided to let it happen when it happened. The birth of a second child changes the dynamics of a home yet you are aware of how it works since you have "been there, done that" per say. That was not the case with our second child because we found out at 25 weeks of pregnancy that our second son would be born with some serious health challenges. Jeremiah David was born, July 31, 2001 the same weekend we opened New Life Worship Center. We did not share any information with family or friends until after Jeremiah was born. We were told he had an enlarged left kidney, he had a hole in his heart, and the most dismantling news he was missing his corpus callosum.

The corpus callosum is the part of the brain that is made up a millions of neurons that connect the left hemisphere to the right hemisphere of the brain. We were told that Jeremiah's corpus callosum was partially there or not there at all. The final diagnosis is that he could be a college graduate or he could have extreme mental retardation we would have to wait and see.

So can you imagine, having a rambunctious two year old son that is healthy and now a baby boy born extremely ill. We brought Jeremiah home from the hospital unaware of what the future held for him and our family. We were introduced to a new world of doctors; a cardiologist, urologist, genetics expert, pediatrician, neurologist, and an assortment of therapists. How do I as a man handle the "pressure" that comes with a child that has special needs? In the beginning it was very difficult for me to digest. I dove into getting the new church up and going, which caused me to be less visible at home. When I reflect back on those first three years, I now see that was my way of dealing with having a sick child. I wanted to work so that I could provide the best quality of life for him but that caused me to sacrifice one of the most important elements in his development, spending quality time with him.

My wife handled all the doctor's appointments, medications, and childcare. I didn't see her break down much, but I found out later as the years passed that she often had her moments, it was just something she did when she was alone. At first, I wanted to try and "fix it" that is how I am wired, if there is a problem in my family with my wife and children I am going to try and fix it. Well, I could not fix this; all I could do was trust God and support my wife. There were many days when I broke down and cried like a baby, "Why God, why my son?" I can't say that I got an answer but I do know that Jeremiah has taken my faith in God to a level that I never dreamed possible. My wife and I must "walk by faith and not by sight". We stand daily on Hebrews 11:1.

*Now faith is being sure of what we hope for
and certain of what we do not see.*

As the years progressed we shared more with family regarding Jeremiah's diagnoses. We were also very open with our church about our son so they could pray for us and understand the developmental delays that he began to display. At the age of two he could not walk or talk and he did not have any teeth. Therapist came to the house to work with him through the states early childhood development program entitled First Steps. Jeremiah captured the hearts of everyone because he loved to be held and he loved to kiss. My wife takes great pride in making sure our kids look nice.

At the age of three Jeremiah had his first "grand mal" seizure. This type of seizure can kill you if it is not stopped with a rectal medication. I remember the first seizure Jeremiah had because it was on a Sunday morning. My wife was awakened by Johnny who carried Jeremiah downstairs which was unusual. This morning Jeremiah was not making any noises Johnny just saw him in the room awake and carried him down stairs at the age of five. When Alicia saw Jeremiah was not responding to her voice she began to pray because she knew something was wrong and she called

911. She had been researching Jeremiah's disability on the internet weeks prior and saw that many of the children have seizures, so with this abnormal response that day she knew that was the problem. I was able to make it home right after the ambulance left the house. They had accidently left my wife, so she was there to tell me "go back to preach" the devil is not going to get the victory; our son will be fine, go do what God has called you to do.

I don't know how I did it but I did go back and finish the services that day. Jeremiah left the hospital with medication to control the seizures and we left with a new level of faith because his seizures are connected with sleep. What does this mean? It means we have to pray that God will keep our son during his sleep so he doesn't wake in a seizure. There have been countless times that he just so happened to be in our bed and he wakes my wife or me because of his twitching, or the slight clicking noise that his mouth makes during the seizure. We immediately begin praying and follow the action plan that the doctor gave us. Praise God, he has only been to the hospital emergency room three times in his nine years of life. You are probably thinking that after the seizure began my wife became a stay at home mother but she is not. Her way of staying balanced was to work full-time along with the fact that she had great health insurance which allowed us the best quality of care for Jeremiah during these early years.

When you are raising a child with special needs medical expenses can cause great burdens for the family. We saw her medical insurance and my secondary insurance as a blessing. In addition we were also able to afford a full-time caregiver so that Jeremiah would not have to attend daycare but the therapist could come to our home and work with him. We are a team when it comes to Jeremiah's care! We decided that as God continues to bless us we will make sure Jeremiah is exposed to many different opportunities in his life. He has already been on two cruises, to Disney World numerous times, he has seen every major Gospel recording artist (he loves gospel music), he has flown to California, Texas, New York, and we have given him every therapy that we know that will benefit him to become a productive citizen in life. We know that if we do everything that we can do in the natural then God will do the "supernatural" to complete the healing in Jeremiah's body.

We share parenting responsibilities so that neither one of us becomes overwhelmed. Statistics show that parents with special needs children have a higher divorce rate than the national average. Many people sacrifice their purpose and calling when they have a child born with special needs, I believe this causes great tension in the marriage and causes resentment in the home. Some things that we have done to keep our family well-balanced; we have found a non-profit organization National Disorders of the Corpus Callasoum, that has connected us with families that have children with the same disability. Once a year we attend their conference as a family vacation so we can meet new families and attend workshops to learn more about Jeremiah's condition. We had to realize that we couldn't do it all by ourselves but we had to allow God the ability to send us help. Even though Jeremiah goes to school full-time we have three ladies and also my mother that help us with the children. They call themselves "Team Ramsey". My wife and I can have date nights, attend conferences without the children, and attend Johnny's athletic events because of the support.

I know you are wondering, why in the world they would adopt a child with such busy lives and a special needs child. Well, we often asked ourselves the same questions before we made the final decision to do so. In 2005, my wife began talking to me about adopting a little girl. She spoke about it often during our marriage but I really didn't see how we could do it. To be honest, I shot down the idea by asking was she going to stay home full-time with the kids. She was not ready to do that so that would end the conversation. As time went on we just moved on with our careers and parenting our two boys. Alicia no longer discussed the idea and she began to emerge herself in her career. The church was growing and I was becoming more interested in other ministry opportunities. Our life was good but it was not complete.

In 2007, I had a friend that lived in town and he shared their stories about being adoptive parents. He and his wife were also parents of a special needs child. I remember talking to him about my wife's desire to adopt and he encouraged me to do so. He told me how his special needs son matured when they adopted younger siblings. I had never seen it from that perspective before. He ended the conversation by saying there would not be a "great" time to do it, you just to do it. I encouraged my wife to move forward again with it but this time she had reservations because she did not see how this could fit into our new life styles. I was now the pastor of a church with multiple services several times a week and she was now a principal. She did agree with me to do some investigating, so we sat down with an adoption agency to find out how it all worked and if it was something that we really wanted to do. So, we moved forward and then stopped again when we found out the difficulty in having a "sex specific" adoption because we knew we wanted a daughter.

Now it is 2008 and the adoption plans are once again on hold. In October of each year Bishop Dr. I.V. Hilliard has an annual conference in Houston, TX that we attend. This particular year, my wife took a couple of days off work so she could attend the conference with me for the entire time. One evening while we were at a dinner hosted by Bishop Hilliard and Dr. B, we were sitting at the table with a lady that we did not know. This lady use to work for a well known female evangelist and was now working in her family church. She was very kind and enjoyed talking to my wife about her family. During the conversation I left the table and when I returned my wife had a very strange look on her face. She told me to sit down, so she could tell me what this lady just said to her. The lady said she saw me minister on The Word network and she remembers me speaking about our special needs son. My wife confirmed that was me on the broadcast. The lady began to talk about how Jeremiah's testimony was going to make a great impact for the kingdom and in our ministry. She then went on to ask about our daughter. My wife told her, we don't have a daughter. The lady then said, "You are supposed to". She said that your daughter is going to do something special in the life of your son with the special needs and she is going to do something special for you. I always tell our congregation that prophecy is conformational not directional. This prophesy was confirmation and we immediately began the adoption process again when we returned to Indianapolis that was October of 2008.

We decided to use a smaller adoption agency and the doors began opening immediately. We were chosen by a birth mother that was due in March of 2009; my wife and I agreed that was too soon for us. Then we were selected by a second birthmother but she wanted an "open adoption" with visitations and that is something we didn't want. My wife and I were amazed because we have heard of people waiting for years to be selected by a birthmother and/or those who go overseas because they cannot connect with a birthmother here. Here we are new to the process and within the first six months we were selected by not just one but two birth mothers. We later discovered that there were not many African-American families adopting through private agencies. Most adopt through family or the foster care system.

As we entered the summer of 2009 my wife and I sat down to talk about her transitioning out of her career and into a full-time position at the church. My wife is not a "stay at home" type of woman which is fine with me. When I met her she was working two jobs so I knew the type of work ethic she had from the day that I met her. I knew that having her work with me at the church would give her more flexibility, it would be a great help to me in the ministry, and it would help keep the balance in our family with the addition of a new baby. She was hesitant but she knew that it was a must in order for us to expand our family and keep up with the boy's hectic schedules. It was a difficult decision for my wife to make after 15 years in public education but with my support she willingly sacrificed her demanding career for our family. I find myself ministering more and more about "selflessness" in marriage and in parenting. You cannot be a good parent and selfish. It is not longer "about you", what "you" want, and/or what "you" need, it is WE!

Alicia submitted her letter of resignation in July of 2009; the next month we received an e-mail that another birthmother had selected us. She was only forty minutes away and she already had three children, this would be her fourth. I remember the phone call we made from my church office. After speaking with the young lady, she decided she wanted us to adopt her child and we scheduled a time for us to meet. We decided to incorporate Johnny and Jeremiah in our decision to adopt. Johnny was honest and didn't know how we would handle Jeremiah and a new baby. It was hard for him to process his mother not working 60 hour a week anymore and having more time for another child. We felt that if we took them with us to meet the birthmother too, that would help him understand the process of adoption. We showed Jeremiah pictures of babies and talked about it a lot in the present tense.

It was a Saturday in October and we drove as a family to northern Indiana to meet the young lady that was carrying our soon to be little girl. We spent the time talking about her, the children, and her current living situation. We agreed to a "semi-open" adoption. That means no visitation but my wife will send pictures and updates periodically. At first friends and family did not understand this type of adoption, but they now realize it was a blessing because this openness gave my wife the opportunity to learn about her family history and attend doctor appointments. The birth mother told the social worker that she knew we were the right family because we showed so much concern for her and not just the unborn child. The birth mother was so touched by our communication and concern that she invited us to be in the delivery room. She told my wife that she felt more like a surrogate mother and she was happy to give us our "little princess".

On January 7, 2010 it was around 12 noon. Indianapolis had just got hit with the first real snow storm of the season when my wife got the call that our little princess was on the way. This was unexpected because the baby was not due until late January early February. My wife had a beautifully decorated room (pink everything) and a closet full of clothes but no car seat. She rushed out in the storm and purchased a car seat. We both packed clothes and headed to the town where she lived so we could be close to the hospital. It was a false alarm and we ended up staying at a hotel for three days because my wife did not want to take a chance on missing the birth of our daughter. The birth mother felt comfortable calling my wife directly so my wife ended up updating the social worker on the process as we waited in our hotel room for our baby to arrive. On January 9, 2010 around 1:00 p.m. they induced labor and our daughter was on the way. We hung out in the delivery room with the birth mother and her sister. It was a very pleasant environment; you would have never thought the young lady on the delivery table was about to give her baby away to people that she just met three months prior. It did feel as if she was carrying our baby for us because there were no signs of sadness. When it was time to push my wife held one leg while I waited outside the door. My wife said she only pushed three times and our daughter came out.

Judah Maree Ramsey was born January 9, at 6:30 p.m. When the doctor asked who to give the baby to first, the birthmother said her mom and pointed to my wife. I know it sounds like a movie but that is what happens when God puts your divine connection together. I then came into the room and I must admit when I saw Judah tears poured out uncontrollably because it was just so unbelievable to me. We had a daughter that was healthy and beautiful. The hospital was adoption friendly and allowed my wife to stay in the hospital to care for Judah. I returned home after one night in the hospital to spend time with the boys and bring them to the hospital to see their mom and new baby sister. Johnny tells the story now that he wasn't sure about adopting a baby but when he saw her in the hospital he didn't want to leave her.

The birth mother did not give our baby another name, she allowed us to name her. She only asked to see the baby once before she left the hospital so her birth children could meet the baby. It was such a divine connection that everyone, including ourselves, is amazed at how much Judah looks just like my wife and youngest son. After we brought Judah home, I did forget how much work it would be for my wife. I feel like even though she was here, she was not here. She couldn't attend church for six weeks and the baby took all of her attention. People ask why you didn't try to have another child or were you afraid that another birth child would be born with challenges. I would say "no" to both questions because this process of adoption has been a blessing for so many people outside of our family. We lived our life as an open book so our congregation could see that children are a blessing and God has blessed us with the ability to extend our family. We have decided to give a baby girl a life that she would not have been able to have with her birth mother; a Christian home, financial stability, both parents, and brothers that love her dearly.

Are children a blessing a burden? If you believe them to be a burden then you need to go to the Word and examine what your responsibility is and rid yourself of those thoughts. If you believe, however, that the children are a burden in a positive sense, then you "get it". Pastor, you have totally confused me now???? What I mean by this is the burden is a blessing! This is not double talk, it is the truth. God says you have a burden (responsibility) to raise and love the children and this burden should be considered your blessing. Many married couples long to have children and can't. If God has blessed you with the burden of children, whether biological or not, take the blessing and thank Him each day for the opportunity to care for the gift He has given you.

Know that with the gift God has provided there comes the responsibility of His word;

Psalm 78:5-6
He decreed statutes for Jacob and established
the law in Israel, which he commanded our
forefathers to teach their children, so the

*next generation would know them, even the
children yet to be born, and they in turn would
tell their children. They would put their trust
in God and would not forget his deeds but
would keep his commands.*

One blessing of a heavenly marriage is God granting us
the burden of raising his children he has given us. So, are
children a blessing or a burden? The answer in a marriage
from Hell is they are only a burden; in a heavenly marriage
is a resounding, YES, because they are both.

DISCUSSION/APPLICATION

1. How do you affirm your children? If so how and why is that important?

2. How do you show your children that they are loved?

3. How do you set goals for your children and their responsibilities to the family?

4. If your child needs discipline, how do you achieve the desired results?

5. How do you celebrate the unique characteristics of each of your children?

6. What do you do on a daily basis to be sure your children are growing in their faith walk?

7. How do you model to your children a heavenly marriage so they will be able to take it to their own marriage?

Pastor John F. Ramsey, Sr.

Pastor John F. Ramsey, Sr. is the gifted and anointed Senior Pastor of New Life Worship Center, an exciting and rapidly growing church located in Indianapolis, Indiana. Pastor Ramsey attended Fort Wayne public schools and graduated from Snyder High School. Following graduation, inspired by his love of athletics, he accepted a football scholarship at Miami University of Ohio and began pursuing a major in Education. Fully expecting to become a school teacher, he began ferociously studying to become an extraordinary educator. During his junior year at the age of 21, while experiencing the overwhelming power and love of God, he accepted God's Call to the Ministry. It was during these college years that he began readying himself to do the Will of God on a full-time basis.

A dynamic preacher, prolific bible scholar and teacher, and a visionary leader, Pastor Ramsey boldly and unashamedly proclaims Gospel messages to encourage and empower God's people. He ministers with power and prophetic anointing while using humor to make often complex biblical concepts enjoyable, simple, relevant, "down-to-earth," and practical. With an uncompromising and clear mandate from God found in Matthew 28:18-20,

"Therefore go and make disciples of all nations, baptizing them in the name of the Father and of the Son and of the Holy Spirit, [20]and teaching them to obey everything I have commanded you. And surely I am with you always, to the very end of the age," Pastor Ramsey developed a central theme for New Life Worship Center: **A Local Church with a Global Vision**. Pastor Ramsey and the New Life Worship Center family are fully positioned to reach God's people on a local, regional, national, and international basis.

Prior to serving as Pastor of New Life Worship Center, Pastor Ramsey founded and began pastoring the Victory Christian Center, a small storefront church located in the inner-city of Indianapolis. Starting with just one member, Victory Christian Center grew into a strong congregation within seven years. Under Pastor Ramsey's leadership, the congregation purchased a church site and paid off the mortgage within a three-month period. Pastor Ramsey's dedication, commitment, and love of Victory Christian Center moved God's Heart to provide for Pastor Ramsey to open the doors of New Life Worship Center on August 5, 2001. Under his dynamic and visionary leadership and to accommodate its magnificent growth, New Life Worship Center moved from its initial 350 seat sanctuary (Kessler location) and ultimately into a new main location, a 13-acre 80,000 square feet 1,400 seat facility, in the city's historic Traders Point neighborhood in July 2005. Since inception, the church has grown to over 4,500 members with 30 active ministries. To more effectively serve the Indianapolis community, in 2007 New Life Worship Center also completed the *CASH* purchase of a central campus location in Center Township located at 3425 Boulevard Place. Pastor Ramsey serves as mentor and spiritual father to a number of local pastors. He is blessed to serve with Bishop I.V. Hilliard of New Light Christian Center, Dallas, Texas as his spiritual father. Pastor Ramsey is a much sought after preacher and a featured national keynote speaker for various leadership and development programs. God's anointing has enabled Pastor Ramsey to bring some of the nation's leading pastors, teachers, and recording artists to New Life Worship Center to bless the congregation and the Indianapolis community each year.

Pastor Ramsey is a member of the Board of Directors of the National Organization of Disorders of the Corpus Callosum, a national organization whose mission is to enhance the quality of life and promote opportunities for individuals with disorders of the corpus callosum. This organization strives to raise the profile, understanding and acceptance of these disorders through research, education, advocacy and networking. He also is a member of the Association of Independent Ministries.

Pastor Ramsey is most passionate about helping families to become stronger. He is known for his anointing in the areas of faith, relationships and financial stewardship. He is currently working on his first book about relationships entitled, "A *Marriage Made in Heaven, But Going Through Hell*." His previously published books include "*Smart Money Management: A Biblical Approach to Financial Stability* and "*Armed and Dangerous: Equipping Leaders for Effective Ministry*." He is co-author of a highly regarded book entitled, "*About My Father's Business: Merging*

Ministry & Ministry.
Pastor Ramsey is married to his lovely wife, Alicia and they are the proud parents of three wonderful children-a daughter, Judah Maree, and sons Jeremiah David and John Jr.

CPSIA information can be obtained at www.ICGtesting.com
Printed in the USA
LVOW060241050312

271575LV00002B/4/P

9 780984 287475